Understanding youth and crime

Listening to youth?

CRIME AND JUSTICE
Series editor: Mike Maguire
University College of Wales, College of Cardiff

Crime and Justice is a series of short introductory texts on central topics in criminology. The books in this series are written for students by internationally renowned authors. Each book tackles a key area within criminology, providing a concise and up-to-date overview of the principal concepts, theories, methods and findings relating to the area. Taken as a whole, the *Crime and Justice* series will cover all the core components of an undergraduate criminology course.

Published titles

Understanding youth and crime
Sheila Brown

Understanding crime data
Clive Coleman and Jenny Moynihan

Understanding white collar crime
Hazel Croall

Understanding justice
Barbara A. Hudson

Understanding crime prevention
Gordon Hughes

Understanding violent crime
Stephen Jones

Understanding criminology
Sandra Walklate

Understanding youth and crime
Listening to youth?

Sheila Brown

Open University Press
Buckingham · Philadelphia

Open University Press
Celtic Court
22 Ballmoor
Buckingham
MK18 1XW

email: enquiries@openup.co.uk
world wide web: www.openup.co.uk

and

325 Chestnut Street
Philadelphia, PA 19106, USA

First Published 1998
Reprinted 1999, 2002

Copyright © Sheila Brown 1998

A catalogue record of this book is available from the British Library

ISBN   0 335 19505 9 (pb)   0 335 20004 4 (hb)

Library of Congress Cataloging-in-Publication Data
Brown, Sheila, 1959–
    Understanding youth and crime : listening to youth? / Sheila Brown.
        p.   cm — (Crime and justice)
    Includes bibliographical references and index.
    ISBN 0-335-19505-9. — ISBN 0-335-20004-4
    1. Juvenile delinquency—Great Britain. 2. Problem youth—Great Britain. 3. Deviant behavior—Great Britain. 4. Juvenile justice, Adminstration of—Great Britain. 5. Criminology—Great Britain.
    I. Title. II. Series: Crime and justice (Buckingham, England)
HV9145.A5B76   1998
364.36′0941—dc21   97-47447
                                                                                            CIP

Copy-edited and typeset by The Running Head Limited, London and Cambridge
Printed in Great Britain by Biddles Ltd, www.biddles.co.uk

For Kath

Contents

Series editor's foreword   ix
Acknowledgements   xi

1 **Constructing the other: childhood and youth**   1
   Age and the social   1
   Childhood and the Victorian lament for innocence   5
   Youth and adolescence, masculinity and nation   12
   Conclusion: childhood, youth and exclusion   15
   Further reading   17

2 **Problem youth meets criminology: the formative decades**   18
   Criminology and 'problem youth': a long-term relationship   19
   Early British criminology: causes, correlates and delinquents   20
   Transatlantic crossings: the pre-war American legacy   21
   After the war: the youth obsession revisited   23
   Postwar reconstruction: a 'cult of youth'?   24
   A merging of histories: criminology and youth in the postwar era   26
   Critical criminologies: resolving the paradox?   29
   Presence and absence: voices and silences   35
   Further reading   36

3 **Representing problem youth: the repackaging of reality**   37
   Messengers, messages: the power of word and image   37
   Moral panics and problem youth: the study of media
      representations from the 1960s to the 1980s   39
   A total panic? The media and young people in the 1990s   46
   A totalizing discourse of panic?   51
   Further reading   52

4   In whose interests? Politics and policy   53
    John Macmillan with Sheila Brown
    The languages of youth justice   53
    The advance of welfare: the 1960s   54
    The retreat from welfare: the 1970s   61
    Politicizing criminal justice: the 1980s   64
    Just deserts, false starts: the Criminal Justice Act 1991   68
    Howard's Way   70
    New Labour, new punitiveness?   75
    Politics, policy talk and problem youth   76
    Further reading   78

5   'Punishing youth': victims or villains?   79
    Throwing away the key: punishment, politics, press and the public   80
    Young people as victims I: 'behind closed doors' and wilful
        ignorance   84
    Young people as victims II: the other side of the youth crime coin   90
    The murky waters of golden pasts: accounting for collective
        myopia   93
    Further reading   97

6   Youth and crime: beyond the boy zone   98
    Girls and crime: speaking into the silence   99
    Boy-ness and crime: masculinities   106
    Beyond the boy zone?   112
    Further reading   112

7   Conclusion: listening to youth?   113
    Revisiting the domains of youth and crime: discarding the comfort
        blanket   114
    Disparate histories, enduring themes: the powers of articulation   117

Glossary   120
References   125
Index   134

Series editor's foreword

This is the fourth in a series of textbooks – all of whose titles begin with the word 'Understanding' – which cover important areas of debate within the fields of criminology, criminal justice and penology. The aim of the series is to provide relatively short and accessible texts, written by experienced lecturers and researchers, which will give undergraduates or postgraduates a solid grounding in the relevant area and, hopefully, a taste for the subject which will lead them to explore the literature further. Although aimed primarily at students new to the field, and written as far as possible in plain language, the books do not give the false impression that they are dealing with a simple subject, easily mastered. On the contrary, all the authors aim to 'stretch' readers and to encourage them to approach criminological knowledge and theory in a critical and questioning frame of mind. Moreover, they do not simply summarize the relevant literature but, where appropriate, express their own views and explain how and why they differ from other writers.

Sheila Brown's book provides a comprehensive and critical introduction to the 'youth and crime' debate. She discusses in depth the social construction of childhood and youth, the marginalization of young people, the creation of 'moral panics' about their perceived criminality, and the twists and turns of youth justice policy. Focusing upon Britain, she argues that the 1990s have seen not just a series of moral panics, but a 'total panic' about youth crime, its flames fanned by the media, which has drawn ever more punitive and exclusionary responses from Conservative and Labour governments alike. She also examines two issues which have received little close attention, but which are vital to a full understanding of the complex phenomenon of youth crime: the role played by gender, and the extent to which young people become victims rather than offenders. Her parting message is that young people should be 'listened to' rather than 'silenced and scapegoated'. She writes:

The reframing of 'understanding youth and crime' requires either a dissolution of 'youth' as a special object of knowledge and policy, or an inclusion of young people in the social enterprise through the legitimation of their voices and a recognition of their potential for citizenship.

The first three books in the Crime and Justice series covered penal theory (Barbara A. Hudson), crime data and statistics (Clive Coleman and Jenny Moynihan) and modern criminological theory (Sandra Walklate). Others in the pipeline include *Understanding Criminal Justice and the Penal System* (Mike Maguire), *Understanding Crime Prevention* (Gordon Hughes) and *Understanding Social Exclusion, Crime and Justice* (Loraine Gelsthorpe). All are central topics in the growing field of crime-related studies in universities, and each book makes an ideal foundation text for core courses or modules. As an aid to understanding, clear summaries are provided at regular intervals, and a glossary of key terms and concepts is a feature of every book. In addition, to help students expand their knowledge in specific areas, recommendations for further reading are given at the end of each chapter.

Finally, I must again record my gratitude to Roy Light and John Skelton for the original suggestion that I become involved in editing a series of this nature, as well as to Jacinta Evans, Nick Evans, Justin Vaughan, Joan Malherbe, Pat Lee and Gaynor Clements (past and present staff of Open University Press) for their help in bringing it to fruition. Most of all, I thank the authors, who have all made my job as series editor both simple and pleasurable.

Mike Maguire
Professor of Crime and Criminal Justice, University of Wales, Cardiff

Acknowledgements

Thanks to Mike Maguire for his help and support, and to Justin Vaughan at Open University Press. Thanks to Steve Redhead for reading various early drafts, with patience. Also to Sue Turner for her unfailing willingness to wrestle with the intricacies of information technology, among other things; and last but not least, to all my friends, patient and forgiving as ever. You know who you are!

chapter one

Constructing the other: childhood and youth

Age and the social
Childhood and the Victorian lament for innocence
Youth and adolescence, masculinity and nation
Conclusion: Childhood, youth and exclusion
Further reading

In this chapter we employ a historical approach to demonstrate the origins of present-day perceptions of childhood and youth as 'problem' categories for the adult world. As we move into the twenty-first century, childhood and youth become increasingly controversial and confused notions. In order to understand why this might be, we need to reconsider the nature of these states as they have been constructed historically, and their place within a more general theory of the life course as a social and cultural phenomenon. In this chapter we will also make some inroads into understanding the relationship between concepts of age and concepts of deviance and 'otherness'. Only then can we begin to address, as we do in subsequent chapters, the seemingly inextricable relationship between youth and crime.

Age and the social

Many of us will be used to thinking of the categories of age as fixed and natural. We think of certain attitudes, behaviours or lifestyles as being 'only natural at that age'. We often have taken-for-granted common sense notions about what to expect of childhood, youth, adulthood, middle age, old age and so on. Indeed, it is not to go too far to suggest that when people deviate from the social expectations attached to their age group our sense of social order is subtly outraged. Children acting 'like adults' pose, somehow, a threat; similarly perhaps some of us do not like to see 'mutton

dressed as lamb'. The problem we are introducing here is that in truth, neither 'age' nor 'generation' (Pilcher 1995) are simple or natural categories.

The only 'truth' we have is that we are born, we grow older and we die.
The attributes attached to the intervening years ('childhood', 'youth', 'adolescence', 'middle age', 'elderly', etc.) are largely social. By this we mean
that the expectations attached to age are culturally produced and sustained.
Whether through academic/professional languages (science, psychology,
psychiatry), popular media (such as film, TV, music and the newspapers),
the statements of public commentators or politicians, or the interactions of
everyday life, the individual's passage through society and history – their
life course – is enacted through a web of socially produced notions of age-
appropriate behaviour and identity.

The theory of age as a cultural rather than a natural category is a relatively new field of enquiry in western social science. Developed through
anthropological studies of non-western societies (see, for example, classics
such as Margaret Mead's *Coming of Age in Samoa)*, recent work has
focused on the ways in which supposedly age-appropriate behaviours and
identities are *representations* of how we should feel, and be, at different
chronological points in our life span (e.g. Hockey and James 1993; Pilcher
1995; Jenks 1996). We turn now to consider some examples of these representations and the ways in which they may be *deconstructed*.

How do we think of childhood? How do we think of youth? How do we
think of middle age? And how do we think of old age?

On childhood, Young (1996) captures one essential part of this process
when she talks of 'imagining' age-appropriate behaviour in her discussion
of the murder of 2-year-old James Bulger by Jon Venables and Robbie
Thompson, two 10-year-old boys. We will discuss this important case in
more detail later, and the significance it has had for definitions of crime and
justice. For the moment, the point to focus on is that the Bulger killing was
seen as, above all, an abrogation of *childhood*. How could children behave
like this? The innocent and angelic 2-year-old, horrifically – that is, vio-
lently and 'deliberately' – killed by two boys who were themselves children.
Suddenly, the whole notion of childhood seemed to have changed, and with
it, a sense of belief and stability in the world around us. It is no coincidence
that the journalist David Smith, in his chronicling of the Bulger case, quotes
Jean-Jacques Rousseau's *Emile* of 1762. Remember, Rousseau tells us, that
'childhood is the sleep of reason'; a time of innocence, simplicity, irration-
ality; we should 'hold childhood in reverence' (cited in Smith 1994: ix). The
real violence of the Bulger case is arguably the violence it did to adult
notions of childhood.

Holland (1997) points to the significance of the way in which the mass
media focused disproportionately on Thompson and Venables's viewing of
Child's Play 3, the horror movie series in which Chucky dolls (outwardly
cute and innocent) are transformed by the demon within, upon which they

begin speaking in guttural adult voices. It is not, she argues, so much a question of whether the two boys were incited by *Child's Play* to commit the act they did, but of the sense in which the media coverage fed on the horror dimension of the case: why was the Bulger killing like a horror film come true? Because, perhaps, the media representation of it conjured up images of childhood as no longer innocent, but demonic. Hence, as Holland argues, 'The Exorcist, The Omen, Carrie . . . the Child's Play films, are stories about the nature of child*hood* . . . and have very little to do with actual child*ren*' (1997: 50).

Holland likens this slippage to a 'confusion of tongues' (p. 50) in which the social representation of something (children) is conflated with a cultural discourse which refers to them (childhood). The demonic child implies the loss of the innocent child, and is therefore a threat to adult notions of control and power.

Youth, on the other hand, is contemporaneously *expected* to be an age of deviance, disruption and wickedness. When teenagers behave badly, they are typically fulfilling negative stereotypes about them. We are bombarded with images of idle, anti-authoritarian, subversive – and inevitably criminal – teenagers, as opposed to the minority of well schooled, clean, respectful, sporting and disciplined teenagers; the former of course spending their time hanging around on street corners 'causing trouble', and the latter in their bedrooms doing their homework. One group is destined for the dole queue and the boot camp, the other for college and career. The vast bulk of criminological writing, indeed, has been about these very distinctions (Tierney 1996).

Imagine now a different scenario: middle age. Mid-life is portrayed as a time of maximum respectability, maximum productivity: the age of the solid, respectable, law-abiding citizen. Crime is therefore portrayed as a problem *for* those in mid-life, rather than the middle aged being portrayed as a problem for society. Rarely do we imagine middle-aged people as corporate or white-collar criminals, embezzlers, or orchestrators of sleaze in politics. The fact that most serious crimes of theft and violence are perpetrated by this age group (Box 1983) is concealed by our cultural notions of respectable middle age and our concomitant fear and suspicion of the young.

Certain images also abound about the elderly: that they are – or should be – passive and vulnerable members of society, is illustrated endlessly by press coverage. Hence both the 'novelty' and the 'comic' value of the following:

A judge told two elderly brothers yesterday to make peace in what are their 'few remaining years' after a family dispute ended in court. After giving Maurice Berger, 75, a 30 month suspended sentence for a 'vicious and potentially lethal' assault with a metal bar on his 81-year-

old brother, Judge Timothy Pontius told him: 'Heaven knows, we have
a short enough time on this earth – you and your brother rather less
than most' . . . he told the defendant, who bowed repeatedly when sentenced, 'I am rather more used to dealing with young thugs and
drunken hooligans for offences such as this, not respectable and law
abiding pensioners . . . you could have killed your own brother'.

(*Daily Telegraph* 24 February 1996)

Is, then, this very serious assault, which could easily have ended in death,
in murder, in fratricide, to be treated as little more than a joke?

In order to understand this apparent anomaly in the way in which we
regard the crimes of the youthful and the elderly, we must distance ourselves critically from the assumptions we hold about old age. The crucial
notion here is that of the *infantilization* of old age (Hockey and James
1993). This involves the ascription of child-like qualities such as vulnerability, imperfectly developed reasoning, deficiency in knowledge and understanding, and so on, to chronologically older adults. One of the clearest
illustrations of this in contemporary discourse is in magazines aimed specifically at retired people. Free with *Yours* ('Britain's leading news-stand
magazine for retired people', February 1996) came a 'Tell the Story of Your
Life' booklet: a special 'nostalgic booklet and kit' including 18 stick-on title
lines, 36 decorative motifs, a 12-page 'nostalgic look at landmarks of our
lives' . . . and so on:

Dear Reader,
With the help of this booklet you can re-live moments of your life,
write them down and produce a beautiful book . . . the only materials
you will need to begin is [*sic*] some plain A4 paper (preferably with two
punched holes in one side) . . . Please have a go . . . don't be put off by
feeling you can't express yourself very well, or that your spelling is a
problem.

(*Yours* February 1996)

One could be forgiven for assuming that this is addressed to six-year-
olds. Nauseatingly twee stickers entitled 'My Favourite Things' are inter-
spersed with patronizing instructions and injunctions 'not to be shy'. Thus,
as Hockey and James (1993) show, infantilism 'should' be a property of old
age. Deviance is as much about overturning cultural expectations as it is
about a general conception of right and wrong in themselves; the life
course, as a cultural construction, is no different. Age, more than anything,
is about the expectations – morally and behaviourally – which we place on
a person's chronological positioning in the life span, the sense in which age-
stages are 'conceived and articulated in particular societies into culturally
specific sets of ideas and philosophies, attitudes and practices' (James and
Prout 1990: 1).

As we will see in later chapters, we cannot sensibly move towards a fuller understanding of youth and crime until we jettison our search for the holy grail of what causes the 'youth of today' to commit heinous acts. We need to concentrate on the interrelationship of cultural representations of age with institutionally framed power relationships. Pilcher (1995) emphasizes three essential tasks in considering this question: the historical variability of the notion of childhood, the cultural specificity of notions of childhood, and the analysis of the relationships between adults and children in terms of power, control and dependency (p. 32). We shall attempt to touch upon all three of these dimensions in our discussion below.

Childhood and the Victorian lament for innocence

By tracing some important aspects of the history of discourses of childhood, we may begin to see how this supposedly natural stage has gone through various stages of interpretation and mutation. This, to reiterate Holland's (1997) point, demonstrates the dissonance between adult conceptions of childhood and the real lives of children.

The notion of childhood as a specific, special and distinctive state – as a historical and cultural product rather than as a biological necessity – is typically attributed to Philippe Aries's *Centuries of Childhood* (1973, first published 1960). Although very difficult to distil (the Penguin edition runs to some 339 pages of closely argued historical evidence), his argument is commonly paraphrased to posit that in medieval society, the idea of childhood as we know it did not exist: 'Medieval Art until about the Twelfth Century did not know childhood . . . it seems probable that there was no place for childhood in the medieval world' (Aries 1973: 31).

This is not to say that *children* did not exist, but that the idea of childhood came into being alongside other historical changes. Aries focuses on the emergence of schooling and the transformation of family relationships during the sixteenth, seventeenth and eighteenth centuries as the institutional sites which were crucial in producing discourses of childhood (James and Prout 1990). Children were no longer treated as small adults, but as a distinctive category of beings (see Jenks 1996 for a good synthesis of these arguments).

It was in Victorian society, however, that the 'cult of childhood' reached its height and laid down a marker for all the subsequent debate of the twentieth century on the nature of the child. Nowhere is this clearer than in the proliferation of literature of all kinds both for, and about, children in Victorian society. Alongside the printed word came images, commercial and artistic, educational theories and practices, a burgeoning of markets in the production of special clothes and toys for children, and heated political and philanthropic debate over the special nature of the child (James and Prout

1990; Hockey and James 1993). Thus a clear distance was established between childhood and adulthood. The child was to be protected, trained, but not to have autonomy (Ennew 1986).

With a schizophrenic dualism so redolent of the Victorians, childhood was at the same time idealized, worshipped and protected, feared, regulated and punished, and debased, exploited and appropriated (Hendrick 1990). It is this process that we must first explore to understand the subsequent fate of the notion of childhood in the twentieth century.

Hendrick (1990) identifies no less than five versions of childhood which were articulated during the Victorian era: the Romantic child, the Evangelical child, the Factory child, the Delinquent child, and the Schooled child. All emerged between 1800 and 1880, to be followed by the Psycho-medical child and the Welfare child as life swung into the twentieth century and the Edwardian era (1990: 37–47). Similarly, Jenks depicts the 'natural' child, the 'social' child, the 'Dionysian' child and the 'Apollonian' child (1996). The major point here is that all these different 'versions' of childhood may be identified as reflecting the social conditions of the time rather than as natural or intrinsic qualities of a universal state of childhood.

What, then, were the delineating features of these constructions of childhood (or, one should rather say, child*hoods*) in the Victorian age?

Victorian literature and art depict a romantic and obsessive concern of middle class adulthood with the notion of childhood. The discourse of the Romantic child presents a psychologically disturbing picture, at once emptying childhood of sexuality and knowledge, by imputing innocence and virtue as quintessential qualities of the child; while at the same time making that very innocence and virtue sexually charged. As Hockey and James note, at first glance sexuality and innocence 'make strange bedfellows' (1993: 69). Jackie Wullschlager, in a fascinating essay on children's literature, encapsulates the apparent contradiction in a quotation from the Victorian clergyman and diarist Francis Kilvert. While extolling the essence of childhood as innocence and purity, he noted: 'One beautiful girl stood entirely naked on the sand . . . there was the supple slender waist, the gentle dawn and tender swell of the bosom and budding breasts . . . and above all the soft and exquisite curves of the rosy dimpled bottom and broad white thigh' (Wullschlager 1995: 12).

Wullschlager locates this convoluted vision of childhood in the fantasy of the middle class Victorian man. He was living in a society where the overt expression of sexual desire was castigated, where suppressed desire resurfaced as an obsession with innocence. As Michel Foucault would have it, the apparent absence of sexuality in Victorian middle class culture was always a myth, for sex was everywhere (1990). Nowhere is this clearer than in the case of the cult of the 'Romantic child'. From the personal lives of epochal children's writers such as Lewis Carroll to the paintings of John Everett Millais, the softness, tenderness and innocence of children was the focus of a heady passion. Carroll – lonely, celibate, intellectually and practically divorced from the coarse grain of everyday life – channelled his energies into inventing Alice in Wonderland and photographing 9- and 10-year-old girls in as few clothes as possible.

'At *any* rate', wrote Carroll to a wife of a colleague,

> I trust you will let me do some pictures of Janet naked; at her age, it seems almost absurd to even suggest any scruple about dress . . . My great hope, I confess, is about Ethel . . . If the worst comes to the worst, and you won't concede any nudities at all, I think you ought to allow all three to be done in bathing drawers, to make up for my disappointment.
> (cited in Wullschlager 1995: 37)

The importance of these constructions of childhood is not so much whether we consider (from the vantage point of the twentieth century) figures such as Carroll to be 'paedophiles', which has been a common critical assumption of the 1970s onwards, but the way in which the 'Romantic' (sexualized-de-sexualized) child had little to do with the lives of young people per se, and everything to do with the nostalgia, longings and social life of adults. Eric Griffiths, Fellow of Trinity College Cambridge, commented in an interview with *The Guardian* (26 April 1996), 'That his writing is paedoerotic in a certain sense is absolutely true. Yet surely the point is that the evidence of the books wanting to preserve the state of being both an adult and a child is stronger than any . . . biographical data could be.'

The narrow outward conventionality of Victorian, patriarchal, middle class official morality, and the rapid pace of social change occurring at the time, formed the conditions for this construction of childhood. It was reproduced in the whole genre of the Victorian literary idealization of childhood, whether in the figure of Charles Dickens's Little Nell, or in moral stories in the flourishing periodical market of innocent children on their deathbeds. Similarly, the use of childhood innocence as a way of idealizing high rates of infant mortality (s/he has gone to a far better place, atrophied in innocence and uncorrupted by becoming an adult) preserved the Victorian middle classes from the harsh realities of the world they were creating.

They lamented, because this very world – the heyday of industrial capitalism and empirical science – was also a world where machines mechanized the people who worked them, the town overgrew the country, and the secular ousted God. As Murdock writes, referring to the 'archaeology of popular anxieties',

> As Nineteenth Century observers knew very well, the dynamics of modernity called all pre-existing moral and social relations in to question. As Marx put it in 1848 . . . there was an 'uninterrupted disturbance of all social conditions . . . all fixed, fast frozen relations are swept

away . . . All that is solid melts in to air, all that is holy is profaned . . . What Marx celebrated as a liberation others mourned as a loss. They saw established and social restraints crumbling away. They were haunted by the spectre of moral decline amidst material plenty.

(Murdock 1997: 70)

Childhood became one reference point among many in which the tensions and contradictions of the age could be managed and anaesthetized. It was paralleled in an idealization of womanhood, an idealization of the rural idyll, and a lament for lost simplicity. As we will argue later, it is this adult nostalgia and fear which is projected onto the lives of young people. This will be seen to form a recurrent theme in the way in which we have responded to childhood and youth throughout the twentieth century, and which, as we shall also argue, has informed adult society's largely irrational responses to the 'youth crime question'.

What of the other Victorian 'childhoods'? The 'Factory child' is, of course, the inverse of the 'Romantic child'. Contemporaneously with the world of childhood innocence, masculine middle class fantasy and longing, and the cosy world of the nanny and the nursery, as many as 80 per cent of workers in English cotton mills were children (Muncie 1984: 31). Muncie provides a clear account of the construction of the 'Factory child'. In the early stages of English industrialization, child labour was both commonplace and economically necessary. Without the employment of children as young as 5, families would have starved and profits would have dwindled. Not here had children ceased to be regarded as small adults. Economic vicissitudes would not have permitted it. Until the 1830s, argues Muncie, 'the use of child labour remained unquestioned, not only by families who relied on their income, but also by factory owners who were keenly aware of this ever increasing source of cheap labour' (1984: 31).

A number of factors affected the subsequent history of the factory child. Economic and technological developments in production processes were one important dynamic. Manufacturing industries became concentrated in urban centres, the size and complexity of machinery increased, and the division of tasks within the production process changed. Whereas in the early stages of industrialization, production had more nearly mirrored family structures, with whole families being employed as units, the Victorian era saw the breakdown and anonymization of tasks. Children were increasingly seen as too small and too little skilled to take a full part in the production process. Parallel with these developments were the growing strength of a Labour movement dominated by adult males, which sought to preserve wages from the downward pressure of cheap child labour, and a swelling religious and philanthropic movement based in the middle classes which sought to save children from the debasement of factory life in the interests of civilization. Hendrick notes the appalled reactions of middle class reformers to the impact of industrial urban manufacturing, and particularly to 'the violence which it was felt was done to the nature of "childhood" itself; the Factory child seemed to symbolise profound and often little understood changes in British society, changes which seemed to threaten an imagined natural order' (1990: 40).

The innocence of 'Romantic' childhood and all that it stood for, was seen as under siege from the brutalization of children. Most importantly, the state of childhood gathered force as a barometer of social order, linked as it was to the cult of the domestic ideal. Civilization and social order were seen to inhere in the Christian, disciplined, family life of the middle classes where the woman was portrayed as the 'angel of the hearth' and the patriarchal, authoritarian but benign, father the guardian of his 'castle'. The reconstruction of the 'Factory child' was thus born of forces of social class, gender and religious belief, as well as more purely technical or economic imperatives.

These kinds of forces are well portrayed in the literature of the time, particularly in the writings of philanthropists and novelists such as Elizabeth Gaskell, who depicts explicitly and with passion the perceived effects of factory life upon the social order. The Factory Act of 1833 is commonly cited as the watershed of these developments. The 1833 Act virtually prevented the employment of children under 9, and limited working hours for those aged between 9 and 13. Subsequent Acts throughout the century progressively marginalized children from the workforce and the centre of economic production (Pinchbeck and Hewitt 1973 – cited in Hockey and James 1993) and reinforced the notion of the child as 'other' and 'special'. By the late 1840s, revolutions in Europe had also strengthened the middle class conviction that the very social order of England was under threat from brutalization. Gaskell wrote in the preface of the 1848 edition of *Mary Barton*,

> If . . . the woes, which come with an ever returning tide-like flood to overwhelm the workmen in our manufacturing towns, pass unregarded . . . it is an error . . . bitter in its consequences . . . the idea which I have formed of the state of feeling among too many of the factory people in Manchester . . . has received some confirmation from the events which have so recently occurred among a similar class on the continent [i.e. the 1848 revolutions].
>
> (Gaskell 1981: 38)

This must be linked into the transformation of public space and the spectre of the mass or the crowd. The overcrowding of the rapidly expanding urban conurbations (such as Manchester, where Gaskell was writing), the relatively short distances between the houses of the bourgeois and the poor, produced fears such as those voiced by commentators such as Matthew Arnold, of a 'vast residuum', a murky mass, of people outside the bounds of respectability and control (cited in Murdock 1997: 71).

In the unnatural child, the brutalized child, lay the terrifying potential for these 'dangerous classes' to reproduce themselves. Schooling came to be seen as the only hope for the salvation of civilization. Alongside reforming zeal came educating zeal, as the middle classes came to perceive that with the exclusion of children from factories, the Devil would be rapidly making work for their idle hands. No longer fully enclosed within the factories, the children of the labouring poor would be spreading the seeds of disorder and debauchery on the streets. The increasing numbers of street children, child prostitutes and beggars consequent upon the changes of the 1830s became the next spectres of urban life:

> In 1848, Lord Ashley, veteran campaigner for factory reform, referred to more than 30,000 'naked, filthy, roaming, lawless, and deserted children', in and about the metropolis. Edwin Chadwick warned of such children's 'perpetual tendency to moral as well as physical deterioration' . . . In 1840 police in Manchester reported that 3,650 children were sleeping rough in the city.
>
> (Cockburn 1995)

While the prisons became a repository for some – Muncie (1984) notes that in 1835 nearly 7000 young people were in prison, and in 1853, 12,000 – this could not form a practical solution to child regulation, nor did it accord with the idealization of the nature of the child.

That 'solution' arose in the form of the Schooled child, and by extension the Reformatory, or the Delinquent child.

Thus another duality surfaced in the troubled waters of Victorian bourgeois sensibilities; hand in hand, the Delinquent child and the Schooled child began to form (Hendrick 1990). While the notion of 'delinquency' was only fully to take shape with the invention of adolescence later in the century, the writings of the philanthropist Mary Carpenter clearly linked the discourses of deprivation, depravation, social disorder and the need for 'education'. The title of her book, *Reformatory Schools for the Children of the Perishing and Dangerous Classes and for Juvenile Offenders* (1851) is sufficiently clear. Although, as Hendrick correctly points out, the history of the creation of delinquency and the history of education are separate and different (Hendrick 1990: 45) in many respects, the ideological origins of both forms of regulation are similar. Both focused on the special nature of the child; both saw social and physical regulation as integral to the moral health of the child and the moral health of society, and both were ultimately concerned with the symbolic and practical threat of the unregulated child to the sustenance of social order. The discourses of the Delinquent child and the Schooled child came to form the conceptual domains for the construction of the child as 'other' and opened up new public sites for the regulation of childhood: 'there was nothing coincidental in mid-century penologists and social investigators seeking to return children to their true position (to their nature), as it also involved making them more amenable to the class-room' (Hendrick 1990: 46).

This institutional and discursive framing of childhood within the school and the reformatory has had long and profound consequences for the inter-linking of youth and crime. We may juxtapose two excerpts from contem-porary writers – Mary Carpenter and Henry Worsley – to consider the importance of Victorian history:

> The child must be placed where . . . he will be gradually restored to the true position of childhood . . . He must perceive by manifestations which he cannot mistake that this power, whilst controlling him, is guided by interest and love; he must have his own affections called forth by the obvious personal interest felt in his well being by those around him; he must, in short, be placed in a family.
>
> (Carpenter 1853, in Muncie 1984: 37)

> A bane to society, which, like an ulcer on the body, is continually enlarging, and distributing far and wide its noxious influence . . . a general and latent depravity, which a large extent of juvenile deprav-ity seems to indicate, is a state under which the manufacture of a soci-ety must eventually decline, agriculture languish, and commerce disappear.
>
> (Worsley 1849, in Pearson 1983: 157–8)

The construction of the child as a particular kind of social category in Victorian society thus culminated in a series of linked, if often confused and contradictory, conceptions of childhood identity. These focused on the potential and hope represented by childhood to restore a sense of lost order, innocence, and simplicity; and the potential and threat represented by childhood to undermine ideals, moral health and social order.

We encounter here a central dilemma facing the student of childhood, youth and crime. This is the tension between 'fact' and 'myth'. If conceptions of the childhood or adolescent as 'other', 'deviant' or 'threatening' to the fundamental social order could be shown to derive strongly from the general anxieties of (middle class) adults about the nature and pace of change in society – that is, as a projection of adult anxieties – then the validity of the accusations made by adults about the decline in standards of youthful behaviour must also be called into question. It is through exclusion of others that we include ourselves; that we draw the boundaries between the indoor (safety) and the outside (threat), suggesting that there is indeed a 'deeply rooted formation of social fear which presents the vulnerable, suggestible, and dangerous as living outside the stockade of maturity and reasonableness that the rest of "us" take for granted' (Murdock 1997: 83).

The consequence for children's real lives of these constructions is less often considered, and will form an enduring theme of this text. In the 'emptying out' of children's lives and the 'filling in' of adult concerns, crucial directions were set for history whose repercussions have gathered strength, rather than diminished, into the twentieth century. Ironically the quest for the rediscovery of the 'true' nature of the child led to an increasing marginalization and silencing of the actual voices of children. Muncie comments upon this from a class-based point of view, in his argument that the concept of juvenile delinquency did not so much represent a more humanitarian attitude towards young offenders as 'justify an increased surveillance and regulation of both [young offenders] and their working class families' (1984: 40).

Hendrick frames the problem in a more child-centred and 'liberal' way. The school, he argues, 'threw aside the child's knowledge' and required a sense of dependency (Hendrick 1990: 47). The practical benefits of the discovery of modern childhood in some respects, can hardly be contested. This is particularly so in relation to the removal of children from the life threatening physical conditions of industrial labour. But these humanitarian benefits are countered by the economic dispossession of children; enforced and prolonged dependency on adults; the discrediting of their views and experiences; and above all, by ensuring the role of young people as an enduring scapegoat (and contingently a whipping post) for the collective neurosis of a society (Holland 1997).

Thus, as Pearson comments in his lively and detailed history of these developments, the most 'remarkable' feature of early Victorian perceptions of the criminal question was 'the way in which juvenile lawlessness was believed to foreshadow the possibilities of political insurrection amongst the lower orders' (1983: 159).

This extended increasingly, as we trace our history towards the beginning of the twentieth century, to insecurity about the maintenance of British economic prowess globally. This period also sees, not entirely coincidentally, the emergence of the construction of 'adolescence'.

Youth and adolescence, masculinity and nation

The extension of the period of childhood dependency through legislation and institutionalization, and the development of more sophisticated modes of surveillance of the working class urban poor (through philanthropy, schools, the development of police forces and the regulation of popular culture), made children at once more problematic and more visible. It also formed the backdrop against which the development of a construction of youth and adolescence, rather than childhood, was to take place. Indeed, throughout the latter part of the nineteenth century, a number of histories were unfolding which were to have an even greater impact upon the subsequent construction of childhood and youth as 'other'.

Griffin (1993) suggests that we must consider the interactions between discourses surrounding 'race', sexuality, gender, class, nation and age if we are to understand the discourses surrounding youth which were in place by the end of the century. As Wullschlager comments, by the turn of the century, the Romantic obsession with the girl child had been obscured by the Edwardian cult of (male) youth. The broad context here has to be located in the 'impact of Empire'. Harris's statement is hardly too sweeping when he writes that 'British economic and political power in the wider world was in itself a major determinant of the character of domestic society throughout the period [1870–1914]' (1993: 4). Two interlocking developments were occurring during this period. On the one hand, 1870–1914 saw the heyday of the extension and consolidation of imperial power; while on the other, the failure (or refusal) of Britain to restrict free trade and the take-off of German and French industrial capitalism had begun to result in internal insecurities and threats as early as the 1880s (Harris 1993). While Empire reigned abroad, the development of the notion of the masses at 'home' was the order – or rather the disorder – of the day. Despite this apparent 'golden age',

> British society was vulnerable to the perpetual changes and collapses wrought by the collapse of world markets . . . in the 1880s, Britain . . . chose not to protect British home producers against American wheat, with a consequent collapse of . . . rural communities, an explosion of migration to the cities, a rapid rise in living standards for those in secure employment . . . but it could be seen also more diffusely in a certain latent instability throughout the industrial world . . . society was having to adopt to new forms of economic life and thought, long before it had . . . absorbed the social consequences of industrial change and agrarian decline. The result was increasingly a society in which people felt themselves to be living in many different layers of historical time.
>
> (Harris 1993: 5)

Once more the complex insecurities of the era come to bear upon the young; but this time on 'youth' rather than 'childhood'. For the middle classes, education came increasingly to be a focus for the preparation of their sons for colonial rule and trading success; the teenage sons of the poor were concomitantly focused upon as the origin of domestic disorders in the cities and the source of industrial failure. The preconditions for a universalizing discourse of youth were in place: a youth which was either to be the standard bearer and upholder of a Great Nation, or the scourge of the future and the harbinger of doom. In particular, concern was turned to the perceived problem of young men in gangs on the streets. In part, of course, this reflected reality: youthful street disorder formed an aspect of everyday urban life. Some of this may be described as 'political', at least to the extent that it represented the response of the urban working class to the increasing regulation of their lives and modes of popular culture. Since the modern police force itself may be seen in part as the middle class answer to the fear of disintegration in the Victorian city, it is hardly surprising that resistance was generated among those who were to be policed (Storch 1980). More broadly, however, the popular culture of youth, whether overtly political or not, was increasingly regulated in public places, so that by the latter part of the nineteenth century, 'the distinctive styles and subcultures of working class youth were well established as a highly visible, much remarked upon . . . feature or "problem" of the urban scene' (Davis 1990: 44).

Yet again, however, the important point is the way in which youthful behaviour constitutes the locus for much broader fears.

The emergence of the hooligan in the late nineteenth century was thus no historical accident; it was an Irish term for what was seen as an unprecedented eruption of youthful disorder on Britain's streets (Pearson 1983: Chapter 5) which was above all, to be regarded as un-British, and 'the name of the Hooligan . . . provided a crystallising focus for any number of overlapping anxieties associated with imperial decline, material incapacity, the erosion of social discipline and moral authority, the eclipse of family life, and what was feared to be the death rattle of "Old England"' (Pearson 1983: 107).

The·solution to the problem was seen to lie in adopting the methods of the public school used to prepare middle and upper class youth for rule and Empire. The existing system of elementary education, in place since the 1870 Education Act extended schooling to the age of 13, was now seen as inadequate to cope with the growing crisis. Sporting and military languages and practices came to be the clarion call. Again Pearson notes the dualism in this response; for the 'hooligan' was seen at once to be a source of recruitment for imperial armies, and therefore to represent the future salvation of the Empire; and as the threat to its survival as a source of degeneracy and slackness.

Thus Davis (1990) points out that the discussion of hooliganism was explicitly linked to discourses on the state of the nation, the rising supremacy of Germany, and the poor showing of Britain in the Boer War. Imperial anxieties were projected onto youth through the discourse of hooliganism.

It will be of little surprise by now to learn that the response was the proliferation of more institutions for the regulation of young people, further delineating them as 'special' and marginalizing them as 'other'. This phenomenon cannot be understood without reference to the development of social theory and science in late Victorian society, for a powerful alliance in the construction of youth and its regulation was made between social and scientific discourse and social 'reform'.

Within the framework of genetic psychology, G.S. Hall (1904) defined adolescence as a 'physiological stage triggered by the onset of puberty' (Griffin 1993), which concomitantly involved a period of 'transition' to 'normal adulthood' via a sexual 'awakening'. We have come largely to accept these categories as constitutive of some real state of adolescence; what Griffin is able to do in her detailed history of ideas is to show that the emergence of adolescence had as much to do with Hall's own interests and background as they did with the 'discovery' of a new life phase. Hall was concerned to establish psychology as an expanding, medicalized discipline and to shift the emphasis from 'the spiritual and the religious realm to the sexual and biological domain'. This in turn may be seen as part of the general growth in power of psycho-medical discourses in the nineteenth century, attendant upon the influence of Darwinian notions of evolution. It is important to underline at this point the gendered and racialized nature of the concept of adolescence, for here we are able to see how social and scientific discourses danced in step to the music of Empire.

In its emphasis on masculine heterosexuality, Hall's concept of normal adolescence was coterminous with contemporary concerns for the health of the nation: 'one of his main concerns was the need to control masturbation, especially amongst young men . . . homosexuality, especially amongst young men, was also a potential danger which had to be controlled and channelled into "normal" adult heterosexual relationships' (Griffin 1993: 17).

The concern, of course, was not just that 'slack morals' would undermine the backbone of the nation, but the declining birth-rate of the time, and the threat of 'race suicide' contained therein. Women were seen as less of a threat to the nation than young men because they were not seen, in general, as sexually driven or active independently of childbirth; nor was lesbianism recognized. Women were perceived as more naturally obedient to their biological destiny, which was to ensure the survival of the 'race'. The main concern with regard to adolescent girls was to ensure the regularity of their menstrual cycle and in other ways to ensure their physical fitness for childbearing (Griffin 1993).

Hence the categories 'white', 'masculine', 'heterosexual', are moved centre stage as key indicators of the 'health' of adolescence. This had two crucial impacts upon the later development of studies of youth and crime.

Firstly, the subsequent history of the study of delinquency was inordinately obsessed with the behaviour of young white males (their 'normality' after all was to be the indicator of the state of the nation). Secondly, the voices of non-white, non-heterosexual and non-male young people were to become marginalized and excluded even further than those of their white male peers.

Conclusion: childhood, youth and exclusion

The above account charts historically a process of exclusion: the setting apart and differentiation of some social groupings by others. What is notable about processes of exclusion is that they typically involve marginalizing the excluded groups: that is, denying their right to be self-determining, to have direct access to the general forms of power and resources in society, to have a voice in the making of decisions about their lives. Other histories of exclusion have focused on, for example, race or gender; here we have taken the rather less usual focus of age gradation and the exclusion of childhood and youth.

The making special of certain groups by defining them as representing childhood or adolescence, may no longer be seen as simply a benevolent process based upon the special needs of a biologically driven life cycle. The coincidences of history and discourse are too many. That certain young people may have benefited in substantial ways by their constitution through the discourses of childhood and adolescence is not in question. Our concern is rather to identify the senses in which their delineation as 'other' leaves them open to a projective process whereby their own voices are lost and the anxieties and angers of a social formation may come to rest upon their shoulders.

Such exclusion is rarely beneficial to the reputation and status of the excluded social grouping. Theoretical explanations for the tendency of societies and individuals to create a discourse of difference range from the psychoanalytical through the anthropological and the more conventionally sociological. What remains more or less constant through different disciplines and accounts is the threat posed by the notion of marginality. This is fundamental to understanding how age operates in relation to criminality and criminalization.

Mary Douglas (1994) frames her discussion of difference-exclusion-otherness through a study of the concepts of pollution and taboo:

> granted, disorder spoils pattern, it also provides the material of pattern . . . this is why, though we seek to create order, we do not simply condemn disorder. We recognise that it is destructive to existing patterns; also that it has potentiality. It symbolises both power and danger.
>
> (Douglas 1994: 195)

While Douglas is writing here from a somewhat structuralist perspective, writers closer to the psychoanalytic tradition have focused on the importance of exclusion to the maintenance of self-identity. In this sense the stereotype of the bad person enables us to

> split the world into good and bad objects, and the bad self, the self associated with fear and anxiety over the loss of control, is projected on to bad objects. Fear precedes the bad object, the negative stereotype, but the stereotype – simplified, distorted, and at a distance – perpetuates that fear.
>
> (Sibley 1995: 15)

Discourses of childhood and youth as 'projection screens' of adult fear (Davis 1990) need to be considered at both these levels of explanation.

Psychoanalytic discourses, themselves a product of the Victorian age, present us with a form of reflexivity – a kind of self-examination – of that era. Discourses of difference both take away power and legitimacy by denying the importance and competence of social groups to take a full part in social life; at the same time they attribute powers of danger to 'otherness'. We place ourselves in a constant state of ambiguity towards otherness, then, firstly by creating it to ensure our own psychic survival, and secondly by fearing it, as a threat to our survival. In neither part of this tortuous equation can we honestly declare that we are taking seriously the need to understand the groups upon whom our fears are projected. This is the crucial background to understanding youth and crime.

Further reading

James and Prout (1990) is an edited volume which contains a number of interesting essays on the social construction of childhood; see in particular the piece by Hendrick. Pilcher (1995) provides a brief introduction to age and generation in social context. Jenks (1996) is a rather more complex text on childhood. It is never too soon to get acquainted with Pearson (1983) and Davis (1990), both of whom provide essential further reading for this volume. Griffin (1993) is rather difficult, but may be useful to those readers with some background in sociology or psychology.

chapter two

Problem youth meets criminology: the formative decades

Criminology and 'problem youth': a long-term relationship
Early British criminology: causes, correlates and delinquents
Transatlantic crossings: the pre-war American legacy
After the war: the youth obsession revisited
Postwar reconstruction: a 'cult of youth'?
A merging of histories: criminology and youth in the postwar era
Critical criminologies: resolving the paradox?
Presence and absence: voices and silences
Further reading

The task for this chapter is to assess in what ways criminology and some of its associated fields of inquiry – in particular, sociology and cultural studies – have constructed 'youth' through the academe, concentrating on what we have termed the 'formative decades' of the 1920s through to the 1970s. The intention of the chapter is not to provide a comprehensive overview and assessment of specific theories and studies. These are covered thoroughly in the cited textbooks and suggestions for further reading. Rather, the aim is to understand how and why 'youth' became intertwined with the study of crime to the extent that 'delinquency' and 'youth culture' as areas of knowledge production have historically dominated academic fields which might otherwise have displayed much more diversity. Did academia, in its attempts to provide a rigorous method of interrogating the social, transcend the exclusionary and mystifying practices of media and popular discourse? Or did it, albeit using a more elaborate language, reflect rather than challenge the processes we have discussed in Chapter 1? What kinds of links may be made between the unfolding of academic studies and the social contexts of their development?

Criminology and 'problem youth': a long-term relationship

Firstly, it is necessary to make some preliminary comments about the nature of criminology as an academic enterprise. In this section we are concerned to sketch in briefly some of the conjunctions and alliances between academia and wider societal and institutional developments.

It is widely recognized that criminology is an eclectic project, rather than a 'discipline' in the strict sense of the word. Some writers would characterize it as essentially a 'raider' discipline, having no inherent philosophy of inquiry, aims or methods but, rather, drawing on a broad range of other disciplines, including law, sociology, psychology, psychiatry, forensics, statistics, geography – potentially almost any area of academic practice which seeks to make sense of human behaviour (see, for example, Cohen 1988 and Tierney 1996 for a discussion of this). Others, while acknowledging the diversity of the field, would emphasize the unifying themes in criminology – most obviously its concern with crime as an object of study, and within this its use of systematic empirical research as a starting point for understanding crime (Garland 1994). It is not our immediate intention to engage with these debates. However, it is important to understand that 'criminology' does not stand in an impartial, separate relationship to either other academic fields, or to policy and practice. Its history has been one of institutional development within government agencies and academic organizations. It has been concerned in some cases principally to further understanding of the social phenomena defined as 'crime', but it has more often been harnessed to other imperatives – for example, to manage better the prison population, to inform legislation and policies governing the nature of the criminal justice system or social welfare systems, to provide a critique of existing social arrangements, to further particular political ideologies, or even, the cynical may argue, to secure economic security and institutional power for criminologists (see, for example, Downes and Rock 1988; Garland 1994; Tierney 1996). Moreover, and partly because of this, we shall use the term 'criminology' loosely to include the sociology of deviance and the cultural studies of the 1970s, which have had a particularly close relationship with the criminological project (Redhead 1995: Chapter 3).

Above all, we must seek to understand something of the fortunes of academic ideas and the social conditions under which they flourish or perish.

It is with this in mind that we begin to explore the long relationship between criminology and young people. Indeed, it is hardly an exaggeration to claim that British criminology embraced young people with fervour while other areas of potential criminological inquiry lay fallow for most of the discipline's history. White-collar crime, corporate and fiscal crime, gender and crime, race and crime, and police crime could, up until the 1970s, boast only a small crop of publications compared with the vast literature on 'problem youth'. Why should this be so?

We have already seen the origins of this preoccupation in Chapter 1, the construction of childhood and youth as 'other' providing a social and cultural context for the general obsession with the young as a locus of anxiety. Small wonder that this should be reproduced in the academic and developing institutional base of criminology during the twentieth century. Griffin (1993) charts the subsequent story of academic youth research as one of 'bad boys and invisible girls' (1993: Chapter 4), a translation of general anxiety and official concern into a *pathologizing* discourse. A historical conjunction occurred in the early decades of the century between, particularly, the growing strength of the 'human sciences' and the already existing construction of youth as a 'social barometer'. Specific conditions both in the interwar and postwar eras can be seen to feed a relentless strengthening of criminology's focus on youth. Below, we will juxtapose the conventional 'map' of youth and crime with broader historical developments in an exploration of this focus.

Early British criminology: causes, correlates and delinquents

The first conjunction between problem youth and academia began, chronologically speaking, with the influence of biological, psychological and sociological *positivism*. These discourses, notwithstanding their differences, typically sought to explain the origins of deviant or criminal behaviour, utilizing a 'scientific' logic. The primary concern was to identify a group of 'delinquent' young people and to ascertain the dimensions along which key features of their biological makeup, psychological functioning or social environments, supposedly differed from those of 'normal' young people. By identifying and measuring these differences between the normal and the abnormal, it was assumed to be possible to predict the incidence of delinquency within a given population.

Cyril Burt's *The Young Delinquent* (1925) is commonly given the dubious accolade of being a milestone in this type of study. Accounts of Burt's work may be found in Muncie (1984), Davis (1990), Griffin (1993), Garland (1994) and Tierney (1996). Burt's approach, stemming from within a medical-psychological paradigm, was to correlate individual psychological differences between 'normal' and 'pre-delinquent' or 'delinquent' schoolchildren, thereby claiming to identify the causal bases of delinquency. As Garland notes, almost everything was 'tested': 'Biometric measurement, mental testing, temperament testing, and psychoanalytical and social inquiries, together with the most up to date statistical methods . . . its findings were expansively eclectic, identifying some 170 causative factors which were in some way associated with delinquency' (1994: 53).

This must itself be seen within a broader impetus of the growth of scientism in modern western societies – everything may be controlled if only we can measure it – and an administrative concern within state bureaucracies to control deviant populations through a more effective use of policing, punishment and incarceration (Muncie 1984; Davis 1990; Garland 1994). Having its roots in positivism, Burt's study was to prove an academic inspiration because of its method of searching for causal correlates of delinquency and non-delinquency. It therefore marked a watershed because it stretched back to the scientific appropriation of youth in the late nineteenth century (see Chapter 1), and looked forward to generations of subsequent correlational studies into the late twentieth century. Hence, 'The scientific criminology which developed in Britain between the 1890s and the Second World War was thus heavily dominated by a medico-psychological approach, focused upon the individual offender and tied into a correctionalist penal-welfare policy' (Garland 1994: 53).

Young people were to constitute the hapless population upon which much of the emphasis of 'scientific criminology' and 'administrative criminology' was to come to rest. Garland notes the expansion of criminological teaching in universities from the late 1930s onwards, 'catering to the needs of the fast growing social work and probation professions' (p. 54). The title of Britain's first criminology journal, launched in 1950, was no coincidence: the *British Journal of Delinquency* (only renamed the *British Journal of Criminology* in 1960), was the 'official organ' for the Institute for the Study and Treatment of Delinquency based at the London School of Economics (p. 55). The development of academic criminology in the United Kingdom was from its inception inextricably linked with concerns to regulate and supervise the children of the poor through social work, education and the organization of juvenile justice. It was never simply a concern with 'art for art's sake', but had explicit orientations towards social control of populations seen as potentially problematic to the maintenance of social order through what has been termed in the French context the 'policing of families' (Donzelot 1980). Thus from an early stage, criminology was centrally defined by its concern with the very ill-defined concept of delinquency, and with the control of the supposed 'problem population' of the young.

Transatlantic crossings: the pre-war American legacy

Meanwhile, a rather different tradition of research was developing in the United States, most significantly in the sociological writings of 'Chicago School' in the 1920s and 1930s and the work of Robert Merton in the 1930s and 1940s. These were to have an enduring legacy in relation to the subsequent development of British criminology in the postwar period (Pearson 1994; Tierney 1996).

The Chicago 'School' in fact represented a series of often diverse and disparate studies, based at the University of Chicago but also allied to numerous policy initiatives such as child guidance clinics, housing projects and early versions of social crime prevention projects (Tierney 1996: 76). The focal concerns of the Chicago School were initially with understanding the impact of rapid urban growth, economic development and multi-ethnic immigration on residential areas and cultures in the life of the city, particularly the extent to which social cohesion and community might be affected by the spatial dislocations attendant upon such changes. It had a wide-ranging mission centring around understanding the city as a whole culture, using in particular the anthropological method. Downes and Rock summarize this eloquently: 'Chicago sociology was to become the sociology of Chicago itself, a detailed anthropological mapping of the social territories that made the city . . . an exploding mosaic of contrasting social worlds . . . Urban life resembled a phantasmagoria, a welter of shifting scenes and identities' (1988: 62).

For a number of reasons, these very diverse projects often ended up focusing on 'problem youth', a fact which was to have a far-reaching impact upon UK criminology. Firstly, the whole point of anthropological and ethnographic method was to capture the culture of the city as it was lived, using, for example, observation and life-history techniques; only then would researchers interrogate the data from the point of view of more formal or abstract theory. Ironically, however, the emphasis upon these methods narrowed down the scope of the studies and slanted them toward youthful delinquency. This was because in practice, despite the scope of the research interests – gangs, organized crime, prostitution, taxi-dance halls, real estate offices, local newspapers, the rooming house district, hobo-hemia, the central business district and specific ethnic groupings, are all listed by Downes and Rock (1988: 67) as foci of distinct studies – the insistence upon ethnography and life-history interviews made the study of visible cultures of the street – relatively 'undefended' cultures, as Downes and Rock put it (p. 70) – much easier than the study of the powerful and often invisible domains of the business sectors. Quite simply, it was much easier to gain access to groups of visible young people on the streets than it was to infiltrate the crime of the suites.

Secondly, there was a link between the activities of the academic researchers and the practical policy initiatives: funding provided by the policy organizations was to be directed toward the solving of social problems, seen in terms of the 'saving' of problem youth. Thirdly, the focus on an ecological (see Glossary) approach to the study of a city in flux encouraged a concern with the transmission of cultures in the 'deviance-rich' zone of transition, a transmission which was seen to occur through socialization processes among young people themselves and the passing on of deviant cultures from older to younger age groups.

As a result, the far-reaching potential of the Chicago School's study of social change and social processes in the ecological system of the city in general – indeed with 'the human costs of capitalism' – became linked inextricably with a gaze directed at the 'deviant' responses of young people to the exigencies of urban life.

Merton (1993) provided a second avenue of American academic inquiry which was later to become a staple of British criminological textbooks, and which equally fastened upon youth. Contextually this related to an American preoccupation with the potential consequences for social democracy of blocked opportunity structures. Frustrated, lower class young people were seen as the potential seedbed of a threat to the ideological consensus around the United States as the home of the 'American Dream', the land of opportunity for all. The evident inability of many lower class young people to gain access to the 'avenues of success' led Merton, in a reworking of Emile Durkheim's concept of 'anomie' (Pearson 1994) to the disturbing implication that the disjunction between cultural goals and structural means rendered the land of opportunity inherently criminogenic (i.e. 'crime-producing'). Delinquency could be seen as an almost inevitable solution to the strains between the culturally desirable and the structurally attainable.

It was to be these influences which would be most strongly taken up in postwar criminology, both in the United States and in Britain, so that by 1940 the Transatlantic paradigm was already predominantly constructed around 'youth', blinkering subsequent generations of academics as they sought to develop their research by engaging with what had gone before.

After the war: the youth obsession revisited

In the postwar period the American tradition continued with the study of the responses by adolescent boys to inequality, in particular utilizing the notion of delinquent subculture as 'deviant adaptation' (Cohen 1955; Cloward and Ohlin 1960; see overviews in Downes and Rock 1988; Pearson 1994; Tierney 1996; and any number of sociological textbooks). The notion of subculture, despite significant differences between studies, was used to denote the coping mechanisms adopted by lower class young males in a social system which denied them legitimate access to the material and status rewards enjoyed by the affluent. This was not just about money, but about masculinity: 'trouble, toughness, smartness, and excitement' (Miller 1958): a creation of status and hierarchy within the gang sustained through delinquency; a kind of parody of the 'parent culture' achieved through resistance to, rebellion against, or retreat from, respectable middle class values.

A further important resource for UK criminology was to be the critique of this genre by David Matza and Gresham Sykes (1961). Their critique related to the over-determinism of the subcultural theorists, in particular charging them with differentiating too sharply between the 'normal' and the 'deviant'. Matza in particular developed his analysis subsequently in the books *Delinquency and Drift* (1964) and *Becoming Deviant* (1969), where firstly he criticizes positivism (and therefore the notion that 'the delinquent' could be meaningfully distinguished from the 'non-delinquent'); secondly, he attacks the conception of 'becoming deviant' which rests on subtle processes of the everyday interaction of the individual with other actors around him (*sic*). For Matza, most delinquency was not so much a 'statement'; it was usually trivial, and incidental to a broader and far less structured passage through life by young people. Young people, then, sometimes drifted into delinquency in particular contexts and under particular conditions, but their activities were not characterized by an adherence to 'delinquency' as a 'core value'. These critiques, although going some way to challenging the notion of youth subcultures as typically criminogenic, nevertheless continued to add to the intensity of academia's scrutiny of young peoples lives, rendering them ever more visible and ever more defined as the object of criminology's gaze. Again, it was to be youthful delinquency which was to form the resource for the development of postwar British criminology. In order to understand fully the way in which the American studies were taken up and remodelled in the British context, it is necessary firstly to revisit the broader context of postwar Britain and the development of what has been termed a 'cult of youth' (Davis 1990) which provided an all too fertile soil for the ever more vigorous propagation of delinquency studies.

Postwar reconstruction: a 'cult of youth'?

A number of quite specific historical factors framed the extent to which, and the way in which, academic narratives of youth and crime from the US were to be taken up and reworked in the UK in the 1950s and 1960s.

The process of postwar reconstruction had a number of far-reaching consequences, leading, as Davis argues, to the rise of 'youth as a category of particular sociocultural significance' (1990: 86). Davis summarizes these factors as a series of demographic, social institutional and social structural/economic changes which carried both practical and metaphorical significance (1990; see also Lury 1996: Chapter 7).

Firstly, there was a concern with the instability of wartime childhoods, seen as arising from the dislocating effects of war on young children (evacuation, disrupted education, the absence of fathers). Davis cites T.R. Fyvel's classic, *The Insecure Offender*, where it was argued that high rates of teenage delinquency in the 1950s stemmed from 'the expression of a particularly disturbed generation, a delayed effect of the war' (Fyvel 1963: 51, cited in Davis 1990: 89). Once more the barometer of the nation's health preoccupation surfaced in relation to youth. How could Britain rebuild her global position and recuperate from the ravages of war if her youth were hurtling out of control?

Secondly, this interlinked with the focus on education as a pivot of reconstruction. The Butler Education Act of 1944 was a central plank of general social reform under Beveridge, and introduced for the first time a system of universal secondary education and raised the school-leaving age to 15. This further placed young people centre stage and institutionalized further the 'state of youth' within state control. Thus in an interview with *The Times*, Geoffrey Crowther, author of the Crowther Report (1959) which lamented the inadequacies of secondary education, claimed that a 20-year programme of education was as necessary to reconstruction as a programme of railway modernization or the atomic generation of nuclear power! (Davis 1990: 98).

This ideological focus had its parallel in the scrutiny of the youth service (see the Albermarle Report of 1960, proposing a 'ten-year plan' for reform and expansion of the youth service based on the notion that 'the problems of youth' were 'deeply seated in the soil of a disturbed modern world' – Davis 1990: 111). Similarly Mary Morse's study of 'the unattached' concluded that young peoples' 'inability' to join a youth club was no more than part of 'a much wider pattern of unstable behaviour' (Morse 1965: 75, cited in Davis 1990: 112). Indeed, the Albermarle Report itself made explicit reference to 'a new climate of crime and delinquency' and 'crime in affluence' (Davis 1990: 114).

This leads to the third strand in the 'youth obsession': a preoccupation with economic changes and the implications for the adult world of young people as producers and consumers. On the 'production' side, the growth of the technological and scientific sectors of the economy led to calls for trained and technical 'manpower', perceived as lying dormant in the unrealized potential of young people. At the same time, almost full employment, despite the supposed skills shortage, helped fuel a high labour turnover that was seen as further evidence of instability among the young. These labour market factors, allied with the educational debates, produced another 'problem': that of the transition from school to work, which was then seen as in need of support, training, and – again – moral education (see Carter 1966). On the consumption side, young people were also to be highlighted. The notion of affluence in relation to young people, as noted in Chapter 3, formed one more focal point of adult unease about young people. Abrams's (1959) *The Teenage Consumer* has been termed 'the first major study of youth culture in Britain' (Willis 1990: 29). Essentially a consumer survey, this work – both at the time and subsequently – has formed an obligatory reference point in academic youth studies. Although (as Garratt 1997 correctly points out) this study focused upon the role of young people within an expanding cultural sector of the economy rather than young people as a problem, it nevertheless both reflected and provided fuel for a further separating out of youth as a distinct entity: 'young people became set apart simply by their market choices, and were defined in terms of leisure and leisure goods' (Garratt 1997: 145). By the late 1950s soaring disposable teenage incomes provided a mass market for records, makeup, clothes, magazines, and a general explosion of popular cultural activity among young people. This inevitably sparked off a minute scrutiny of youthful lives by adults, specifically in terms of life*style*. Once more this scrutiny produced a 'problem' of young people. Either the young were viewed by adults as passive consumers of commercialized 'pop' culture – which was construed as problematic because of its connotations of brain-washing, the unthinking adoption of the mindless hedonistic values sup-posedly purveyed by the sellers of pop culture – or, if young people were seen as actively constructing popular culture through their appropriation of commercial goods and services in the production of 'style', then this was disturbing because of its implications for subversiveness: a rebellion against 'establishment' (i.e. adult) notions of moral order.

Having yet again made youth stand proxy for the condition of Britain, it is hardly surprising that the impact upon academic study was profound. This was as much so in criminology and sociology as elsewhere, in fact, more so, since the growth of UK universities – itself a product of recon-structionism – bound social inquiry ever more tightly with the concerns of an expanding postwar welfare state.

A merging of histories: criminology and youth in the postwar era

Thus, as Tierney comments,

> An emphasis was placed on the social basis of various defined social problems, among which was crime . . . One striking characteristic of the sociological studies of crime carried out during the 1950s and the first half of the 1960s . . . is that they all concentrated on young people and their delinquencies.
>
> (Tierney 1996: 73)

The Anglo-American academic legacy and the conditions of postwar reconstruction in the UK produced a peculiar concern in British crimin-ology and its associated disciplines with 'problem youth' which was to have a double axis: the enduring 'causes and correlates' school reaching back to Burt, and the emergent 'British subculturalist tradition' of the 1960s draw-ing upon the US studies (Pearson 1994).

While our major focus will be on the subcultural tradition, chiefly because of its huge impact on academic criminology, we must first note that despite subsequent criticisms, Burt's work was never to become quite an anachronism. Griffin (1993: Chapter 4) provides an extensive litany of comparable 'origin stories' into the 1980s. These 'updated' accounts, while utilizing more sophisticated statistical techniques, and in some cases embracing sociobiology and modern genetic theory, nevertheless still have in common with Burt the 'elision of statistical correlations with causal relationships between demographical characteristics and criminal behaviour' (Griffin 1993: 103). Similarly, Rutter and Giller (1983) provide an overview of many psychosocial correlative studies, and Farrington (1994) provides a comprehensive overview of psychosocial correlates in relation to criminal careers developing from Farrington and West's (1990) study of 'delinquent development'.

For present purposes our interest is in the methodological orientation of correlative research rather than in a detailed account of the respective merits and demerits of particular studies. Located within the search for a 'science of causes' (Tierney 1996), the concern of the studies is firmly with the key variables in the propensity to, causation of, maintenance of and desistence from, offending behaviour. It is therefore not of relevance to give a voice to the young person's own account of their lives, for the causes of delinquency are seen to lie either outside the individual – in particular in the family background and the role of the mother – or inside the individual, but out of their control – such as for example in genetic dysfunction or psychological malfunction. Such studies thus distance young people as an object of study, rather than addressing them as meaningful or rational subjects. 'The problem' is one posed *by* the young person for society and for scientific inquiry. Similarly the definition of the 'problem' – delinquency or predelinquency – is not considered as in itself problematic. The question as to why particular categories of young people, or particular kinds of behaviour engaged in by young people, are *defined* as problematic (or anti-social, or criminal) in the first place, is not relevant to this type of study. The conclusion by Farrington (1994) is illuminating:

> As with offending and anti-social behaviour, investigations of the causes and prevention of heart disease often require . . . the identification of risk factors and developmental sequences, and randomised clinical trials to evaluate the success of methods of prevention and treatment . . . It is clear that problem children grow up in to problem adults, and that problem adults tend to produce more problem children . . .
>
> (Farrington 1994: 569)

This has led to the critique that such studies in fact contribute to the construction of youth-as-other rather than in any way providing a critique of the marginalization and scapegoating of young people in society. Griffin, indeed, terms this kind of research 'victim blaming' (1993: Chapter 4). 'Victim blaming', although an emotively charged term, does convey the sleight of hand in such research: adult researchers define 'the problem' (what is anti-social, what is 'delinquent', what is socially unacceptable), relegate young people to a zone of exclusion where they represent 'the problem', and then seek to explain why these young people stand 'outside' of society: without, of course, authenticating the voices of young people themselves.

However, it is the British subculturalist tradition, having its roots strongly in the post-Beveridge liberal desire to advance social progress through an 'understanding' of youth, which was to become the most potent force in the conjunction of criminology and youth.

Downes (1988) captures succinctly the melding of postwar reconstructionist perspectives, the American tradition and the equation of criminology with youth', and is worth quoting in full:

> The appeal of American theory was that it addressed a problem, and seemingly furnished a framework for its intellectual resolution, of the persistent rise in official crime rates despite the appearance of both greater affluence and diminishing inequality in the major Western industrial societies. Anomie theory and its subcultural variants seemed to supply the answer in terms of the frustration of rising expectations among socially disadvantaged youth . . . Research in this tradition corresponded to the social-democratic reformism of the Labour Government in Britain and . . . with the reformism of the Democratic Party in America . . . Sociology was seen as capable of furnishing a 'vocabulary of motives' for delinquency.
>
> (Downes 1988: 177)

It was in fact Downes's own study, *The Delinquent Solution* (1966), which formed a crucial conduit for the meeting of these histories, for as Pearson notes:

> It was not . . . until the appearance of David Downes' 'The Delinquent Solution' . . . that British sociological criminology came of age. Undertaking a thorough review and critique of the North American legacy, and interrogating it against the British experience, this work constituted both a path breaking study of the social and economic contexts of juvenile delinquency in London and a rare example of comparative criminology.
>
> (Pearson 1994: 1176–7)

The real importance of this work, then, lay not just in its academic quality but in its crucial, catalytic role in the subsequent 'development and ratification' of the subculturalist tradition in the UK (p. 1177). In comparable vein, the British 'area studies' of the 1950s and 1960s (Downes 1988) drew upon the Chicago School in a modified sense to focus upon juvenile offending and social deprivation in urban neighbourhoods and

housing areas. Consequently, 'the intersections of youthful crime, subculture, and local definitions of territory have thus been understood as central
issues in both British and North American criminology' (Pearson 1994:
1177).

Thus, reviewing the field in 1988, Downes observed that from the late
1950s through to the 1970s (and including his own 1966 study in this):
'Morris began what became successive plunderings of American sources ...
Britain became the offshore laboratory for the distillation of ideas fer-
mented in the USA' (Downes 1988: 176).

The UK development of US perspectives became in effect a dual-edged
sword in terms of its construction of young people. On the one hand, high
quality ethnographies and carefully designed area studies brought to the
discipline a previously unheard of sensitivity of analysis to the understanding of youth and crime. In particular, its according of primacy and authenticity to young peoples' own accounts of their activity fundamentally
challenged the positivist legacy (see, for example, Parker's *View from the
Boys* 1974); young peoples' voices were to be accorded a sympathetic legitimacy. Studies of 'delinquent areas' were able to highlight the complex
interactions between local cultures, housing policies and local economies
in producing the criminality and the criminalization of young people. These
studies challenged the simplistic notion within the 'science of causes' that
the 'delinquent' could be simply differentiated from the 'non-delinquent'
or that 'delinquency' itself could be seen as a simple or monolithic category
(see, for example, Baldwin and Bottoms 1976; Gill 1977).

On the other hand, however, the feeding on the US subculturalist and
areal traditions continued to lock many studies into a focus on young,
lower class males, and arguably closed more doors than it opened. What of
adult crime? What of young women? What of the mundane rather than the
spectacular? In shackling 'youth' to 'crime' in this way the academe continued to impede a fuller conceptualization of either, and ironically provided a support to the processes of 'repackaging reality' discussed in
Chapter 3. Lacking an explicitly formulated critical framework as to how
and why such young people come to be constructed as 'folk devils' in given
social formations and in particular historical contexts, it is arguable as to
whether such studies are part of the problem or part of the solution.

Critical criminologies: resolving the paradox?

Two institutional contexts in the study of youth crime and youth cultures
were to provide a further 'transposition' (Young 1988: 163) of American
ideas, this time into radical and critical criminologies through the National
Deviancy Conference, formed in 1968 and based around the University of
York, and the Centre for Contemporary Cultural Studies at the University

of Birmingham in the early 1970s. Both groupings were to prove important for the way in which 'youth' was to be constructed.

As with our discussion of the reconstructionist period, an understanding of these requires historical context. This context was framed by two significant and related histories. Firstly, the 1960s saw an unprecedented expansion in the university sector, and of funding for research, particularly in sociology and criminology departments. This produced what has been dubbed the 'fortunate generation' (Downes 1988) of social science graduates who could find relatively easy access into teaching and research posts. The economic transformations of the 1950s and 1960s impacted upon higher education to produce levels of job security and academic confidence which will almost certainly prove unique. Hard to imagine from the vantage point of the late twentieth century, these decades facilitated a massive output from scholars who were themselves young and critical. Allied with this was the mood of student radicalism which produced a fusion between the politics of the left and the nature and content of academic analysis. The 'you've never had it so good' rebels of the 1950s were the new generation of academics of the 1960s and 1970s – or, one should rather say, male academics, a point to which we shall return.

This heralded the formation, firstly, of a 'breakaway' movement in British sociology of deviance which, stemming from a sweeping dismissal of positivism, was to transform the subject area through the activities of the National Deviancy Conference (NDC). While still drawing upon the North American scholars, 'NDC studies (themselves constituting a diverse array of subject matters and personalities) did so in a quite different way. The American influence in this case stemmed principally from the critical approaches of Matza and the 'labelling' perspectives of Becker and Lemert, embracing wholeheartedly a qualitative methodology which explicitly sought to accord authenticity and appreciation to the 'deviant':

> Radical criminology was the main torch carrier against reductionism. It was critical of any attempt to see the offender as a denatured, determined creature without conscious will and was insistent on granting meaning to the act of deviancy. It was, in the vernacular, *appreciative* of the deviant act.
>
> (Young 1988: 162)

'Appreciation' in this sense, however, did not simply stop at the offender's own motivations and accounts; it situated the 'meaning' of the act within the wider social relations of a class society: 'It is that part of the discipline which sees the causes of crime as being at core the class and patriarchal relations endemic to our social order and which sees fundamental changes as necessary to reduce criminality' (Young 1988: 160).

(In fact, the extent to which the NDC scholars approached any sense of a critique of patriarchy is highly doubtful – this seems to be added in to

Young's 1988 memoir with the benefit of hindsight, reflecting much labour in the intervening two decades on the part of feminist criminologists: again, we shall return to this issue later.)

Thus, under the banner of the NDC and the 'New criminology' (Taylor *et al.* 1973) a plethora of studies emerged which embraced a critical analysis of capitalism and emphasized ethnographic methods: 'interpretive sociology on the side of the underdog' (Downes 1988: 177). It is at this point, however, that we are brought to a halt. For, in the list of papers given at the National Deviancy Symposium between 1968 and 1973 (numbering some 69 in total: see Taylor and Taylor 1973), less than five specifically addressed 'youth'. Topics ranged from mental illness to con-men, transvestism to prisons, suicide to pornography, but only Phil Cohen's *Youth Subcultures in Britain* (1970) substantially returned to the ground of young people. Laudable, of course, in the light of our criticism of criminology's obsession with youth deviance, but a clear case of babies and bathwater: precisely where a forceful critique could have been launched against the criminalization and demonization of the young in modern capitalist societies, silence reigned. It seems that criminology was still only interested in young people as problems, not as problematized.

In contrast, the Centre for Contemporary Cultural Studies was to provide a fertile meeting ground for radical cultural studies, criminology and the sociology of youth: it was to be cultural criminology (Redhead 1995) which was to effect the most fundamental transformation of the era. Drawing as heavily on European theory as on North American 'new deviancy' (Downes 1988), it was from the 'Birmingham School' that the most interesting studies of youth were to emanate. Diverse in nature, a key thread throughout the youth studies of the CCCS was an essentially celebratory stance toward youth subcultures, locating them within a critique of capitalist economic structures and ideologies.

Loosely, the starting point for these analyses may be located in Phil Cohen's paper published in the Centre's *Working Papers in Cultural Studies Two* in 1972 (reproduced as a shorter version with an introduction in Cohen 1997: Chapter 2). Utilizing a quite different – and theoretically far more sophisticated – approach to the question of youth subcultures than the former transatlantic models, Cohen argued for 'subcultures' to be seen as a complex symbolic expression of the relationship between class structure, social change and actors' meanings. Based on a study of the East End of London, Cohen charts a series of dislocations brought about by planning decisions in the reconstructionist era. Slum clearance programmes brought about the depopulation of the East End's 'traditional' communities of white working class people to new towns and estates on the outskirts of the area, and a subsequent repopulation through an influx of West Indian and Pakistani peoples (*sic*) into the vacated inner residential zone. This was followed, as the implications dawned on planners (the increasing dilapidation of the central area due to the predominance of private landlords), by further attempts at redevelopment by building new high rise, high density housing on old slum sites in the inner area. What resulted, argues Cohen, was a disintegration of community through the disappearance of communal space and the disruption of kinship networks; high rises represented nothing better than 'prisons in the sky' (1997: 52): 'the working class family was thus not only isolated from the outside but also undermined from within' (p. 52) During the same period, the postwar economic growth in high technology industries, and the accompanying transformation of production techniques to large scale, highly automated plant, substantially eroded the localized trade and craft economies formerly indigenous in the area, compounding dislocation. It was young people who were, according to Cohen, worst affected by these exigencies of capitalist development: lacking the traditional supports and sources of identity of kinship and community, and economically vulnerable and atomized in the new industries, the 'crisis' in the working class community emerged in subcultural form among the young:

> The internal conflicts of the parent culture came to be worked out in terms of generational conflict. One of the functions of generational conflict is to decant the kinds of oedipal tensions which appear face to face in the family and to replace them by a generational specific symbolic system, so that the tension is taken out of the interpersonal context, placed in the collective context, and mediated through various stereotypes which have the function of defusing anxiety . . . *It seems to me that the latent function of subculture is this: to express and resolve, albeit 'magically', the contradictions which remain hidden or unresolved in the parent culture* . . . Mods, parkas, skinheads, crombies, all represent in their different ways, an attempt to retrieve some of the socially cohesive elements destroyed in their parent culture.
>
> (Cohen 1997: 56–7, emphasis in original)

Despite the difficulty (and sometimes downright strangeness – for example the use of Oedipal references) of some of the language and concepts in this work, its departure from former accounts of youth subcultures is clear enough. It locates young people squarely as the victims of wider structural processes in class society, and sees subcultural formations as essentially a positive exercise in the recovery of some sense of community, rather than as a product of 'deviant' personalities.

This orientation was further developed in a theoretical essay on 'subcultures, culture, and class' by John Clarke, Stuart Hall, Tony Jefferson and Brian Roberts in the CCCS collection on the subject, *Resistance through Rituals* (Hall and Jefferson 1976). This again is a definitive piece which merits close attention for the radical way in which it constructs the relationship between youth and culture.

It is here that the theoretical influences of the 'new deviancy' inter-actionist and labelling perspectives are explicitly acknowledged, except operating within a Western Marxist framework (Hall and Jefferson 1976: 5–6). This explains the importance of the concept of hegemony within the work of the school, and is what renders it distinctive. For here, at last, is a clear recognition of the ideological role which the category 'youth' had been made to play in postwar reconstruction:

'Youth' provided the focus for official reports, pieces of legislation, official interventions. It was signified as a social problem by the moral guardians of the society – 'something we ought to do something about'. Above all, Youth played an important role as a cornerstone in the construction of understandings, interpretations, and quasi explan-ations about the period.

(Hall and Jefferson 1976: 9)

In a critique of the notion of youth culture used in the postwar media and policy discourses, Clarke et al. reveal the ways in which the anxieties sur-rounding social change in the era of reconstruction were projected onto young people, thus positioning themselves outside the youth obsession. Instead, they emphasize the importance of youth subcultures as subsets of young people, 'distinctive groupings, both from the broad patterns of working class culture as a whole, and also from the more diffuse patterns exhibited by "ordinary" boys (and to a lesser extent, girls)' (Hall and Jef-ferson 1976: 14).

These subsets were seen to occupy a position of 'double articulation': firstly, as necessarily sharing some values of the parent culture (e.g. 'work-ing class-ness'), and secondly, being subordinated to the dominant culture (i.e. the dominant – hegemonic – values of class society). Dismissing the generalized notion of youth culture as a theoretically bankrupt and ideo-logically loaded one which (as we exhaustively argue in this volume) does little more than reflect the preoccupations of certain socially dominant groups of adults, their plea is for an analysis of the specific focal concerns of youth subsets ('activities, values, uses of material artefacts, territorial spaces etc. which significantly differentiate them from the wider culture': p. 14) in relation to their 'deeper social, economic, and cultural roots' (p. 16). The endeavour, then, is to

replace the concept of 'Youth Culture' with the more structural con-cept of 'sub-cultures', in terms of their relation ... to 'parent cultures', and, through that, to the dominant culture, or better, to the struggle between dominant and subordinate cultures ... we try to show how youth sub-cultures are related to class relations, to the division of labour and to the productive relations of the society.

(Hall and Jefferson 1976: 16)

This theoretical framework, then, formed the broad context (while acknowledging numerous differences of emphasis and intra-critiques within the approach) for a series of ethnographic studies ranging from the 'cultural responses of the Teds' as a defence of 'space and status' (Jefferson 1976) to a critical analysis of young people 'doing nothing' (Corrigan 1976), reported upon in the same volume.

The distance travelled by the CCCS in relation to earlier traditions of youth research, then, is measured by:

1 the adoption of a European Marxist perspective stressing the important role of youth subcultures in the relationship between capitalist economic structures and the domination of 'ruling' ideologies legitimating and supporting these structures;
2 the concept of 'resistance' to hegemonic structures and ideologies through subcultural focal concerns: expression and style as 'resistance through rituals';
3 a detailed attention through ethnographic research to specific forms of cultural expression, rejecting generalized notions of youth culture and the generic 'youth = delinquency' equation.

This was followed later by a more specific concern with the genesis, form and maintenance of moral panics about young people within an analysis of class and race relations, shifting attention to the criminalization of certain groups of young people under specific conditions of capitalism (discussed in detail in Chapter 3 of this volume: Hall *et al.* 1978).

Certainly, in moving determinedly from a focus on 'youth as problem', through the critique of generalized 'panics' surrounding young people as a metaphorical projection of adult anxieties under postwar reconstruction, and in the framing of class society as a problem for young people rather than vice versa, as well as in the insistence on detailed ethnography, the CCCS tradition was important. It went much further in challenging the stigmatizing, generalizing and exclusionary tendencies which had characterized many of the previous forays of criminology into 'youth' (partly, of course, by shifting the focus away from crime, as noted above).

The main problem was that in debunking one set of mystifying practices, the CCCS substituted another: the 'symbolic reading' of young people's lives, accounts and experiences in terms of their 'imaginary' relationship to relations of production has left successive generations of students somewhat agog. The 'analysis' bolted on to the ethnography resulted in statements such as: 'The Skinhead style represents an attempt to recreate through the "mob" the traditional working class community as a substitution for the real decline of the latter' (Clarke 1976: 99).

Quite clearly, it is the ethnographer who is to supply the cultural meanings. Of course, the job of the social scientist is to interpret, which means that all social research is by definition carried out at one remove (otherwise there would be no analysis, only reportage); but carried to the extent where young peoples' own meanings are subordinated to abstract notions of 'imaginary relations' between constructions invented by the same social scientists, any notion of actually listening to, rather than simply appropriating young peoples' voices, recedes very quickly. Willis's *Learning to Labour* (1977), probably the most widely acclaimed study within this genre, demonstrates this problem. Despite a sensitive ethnographic study and an excellent account of the development of oppositional subcultures among schoolboys destined for the factory floor, his attempts to theorize the complex relationship between the boys' own perceptions of their culture and its structural significance leads Willis to the conclusion that they have a 'partial penetration' (recognition) of class relations which finds expression in their focal concerns ('having a laff', for example winding up teachers and more middle class students). The undoubted potential of radical cultural studies for providing an authentic and appreciative voice for young people is ultimately subsumed as 'youth' are made to stand proxy for yet another series of adult longings and preoccupations.

Presence and absence, voices and silences

In conclusion, the lengthy engagement of academics with 'youth and crime' between the 1920s and the 1970s undoubtedly went far in providing a rigorous critique of the construction of 'youth' as 'problem' and 'other'. In approaching questions of economic inequality and cultural exclusion, a legitimizing 'voice' was accorded to the young which was consistently denied in other fields, supported by often painstaking and detailed methodological techniques. Some young people were accorded a 'presence' within criminological analyses which could never have been achieved without the critical distance available to the academe. Nevertheless, massive absences remained, and many voices continued unheard as a result of academia's own preoccupations with institutional success and academics' preoccupations with their own biographies. Beyond the discussions already engaged in this chapter were other, fundamental absences. Most notable were the almost complete characterization of 'youth' as white and male; and the almost breathtaking assumption that adult academics can – and should – appropriate young peoples' experiences in the pursuit of their own (subcultural?) focal concerns. These absences will be addressed in Chapters 5 and 6, where we examine the developing directions and concerns of youth criminology. Before embarking upon this task, however, we turn to a consideration of the construction of 'problem youth' through the popular media and through public policy.

Further reading

Tierney (1996) and Pearson (1994) both provide useful accounts of the development of youth criminology. Downes (1988) also provides a useful contextualized survey of the development of criminology; and Downes and Rock (1988) is, as it claims, 'a guide to the sociology of crime and rule-breaking'. Davis (1990) is important for the postwar context. Some foray into the original 'classics' is strongly recommended: Matza (1964), Parker (1974), Hall and Jefferson (1976), for example, are excellent examples of their genre.

chapter three

Representing problem youth:
the repackaging of reality

Messengers, messages: the power of word and image
Moral panics and problem youth: the study of media
   representations from the 1960s to the 1980s
A total panic? The media and young people in the 1990s
A totalizing discourse of panic?
Further reading

We have argued in Chapter 1 that the states of childhood and youth are socially produced categories, projection screens upon which the fears and longings of the adult world are projected, a locus of the creation of difference and the playing out of adult insecurities under modernity. In Chapter 2 we examined the formative role of criminology in both consolidating and challenging this history. In this chapter we explore the crucial role of media and cultural representation in the construction of problem youth. We will begin with a general consideration of the nature of the relationship between representation and society, followed by a specific consideration of different strands of the packaging and repackaging of 'problem youth'. Finally we will address the question of whether children and young people have any hope of media representation which is not dominated by the 'problem youth' paradigm, and the role which young people are being made to play in the media in the transition to the twenty-first century.

Messengers, messages: the power of word and image

If childhood and youth are social categories, then, as we have seen, they are discursively framed. That is to say, our understandings of those categories are always refracted through the prism of public knowledge about them. In the Victorian era this may have been paintings, printed literature, newspapers, poetry, novels and so forth. These publicly produced 'versions' of childhood and youth have therefore long been at the heart of public perceptions about the 'youth problem'. With the advent of 'saturation media' in the twentieth century, public discourse becomes even more a universalized source of understanding. We should be careful here to note that this is not simply a question of the influence or impact of media representations upon our opinions or beliefs, but rather a broader and deeper question about the relationship between representation and reality in modern societies; about how our ways of knowing about or making sense of the world around us can never be derived simply from direct experience. This state of 'mediated being' is contingent upon that most modern of transformations: the globalization of electronic media. Giddens points out that while the advent of printing was one of the main influences upon the rise of the early modern state,

> when we look to the origins of high modernity it is the increasingly intertwined development of mass printed media and electronic communication that is important . . . the visual images [of] television, films, and videos . . . like newspapers, magazines, and printed materials of other sorts . . . are as much an expression of the disembedding, globalising tendencies of modernity as they are the instruments of such tendencies.
>
> (Giddens 1991: 25–6)

In other words, there exists a complex reciprocal relationship between media and society which cannot be distilled into a simple cause–effect dichotomy. Our very identities, our senses of ourselves and who we are, even who we might or should become, are constantly refracted through media images. This leads to the problem of ever accessing unmediated 'reality' *out there* somewhere, for in modernism, *out there* is always *in here* (p. 27). Distant events on the other side of the world are instantaneously in our living rooms; the Internet scatters its rainshower of web sites across the globe; we may sit in electronic chat rooms and discuss the latest atrocity.

Thus words and images in the public domain are dissolving many of the distinctions between our private subjectivities (our internal selves) and objectivities (or external realities); a kind of media version of the statement that 'you are what you eat'! Some theorists would even go so far as to say that we are engaged in a transition to a state of being where there is no longer much distinction to be made between the virtual and the real, the fictive and the documentary (Kidd-Hewitt and Osborne 1995: Chapter 2). A vision of constant 'inter-textuality' is invoked, whereby fiction becomes embedded in 'factual' television programmes (e.g. *Crimewatch UK*) through dramatic conventions such as crime reconstructions: real trials become mass drama through televised trials and the coverage of the trials subsequently affects the 'real' legal process. The entertainment value (e.g. the macabre, the voyeuristic, the violent) of human suffering infuses the movie genre, while the movie genre infuses the presentation of news (Kidd-Hewitt and Osborne 1995: Chapter 2) In this constant blurring of boundaries, the misconception that the representation of childhood and youth could ever have been a simple reflection of the 'real', is finally laid to rest (Jenks 1996).

If taken crudely, these kinds of approaches to the importance of the media could of course end up by implying that the mass of individual human actors are little more than zombie-like creations of global totalitarian forces, a kind of orientation for which the much earlier writings of the Frankfurt School were correctly criticized (Inglis 1993). They could also be misinterpreted as giving credence to the 'video-nasties-cause-children-to-murder' species of moral panic (Barker and Petley 1997). The key to avoiding such misinterpretations lies in the notion of reciprocity; for no media representation is passively received by a mere audience. Whether reading, listening, watching or typing at a keyboard, we are engaged in activity. Consumption is *active* by definition. It requires choice (to take part), interpretation (to create an understanding from the word, image, etc.), comprehension (to produce an overall pattern of understandings from the interpretative process), and so on. We may be what we eat, but we do not eat, taste or enjoy without the cultural and subjective meanings which we place upon eating. In turn, of course, the words-images so consumed further add to our bank of meanings with which we confront the next word-image . . . and so on! Hence, what is required in an understanding of the representation of childhood and youth is, firstly, an inquiry into the kinds of reciprocities involved between the media and society: why is it that certain representations are popular, powerful, influential? From where do they gain their popular power? Why are certain types of content and images selected over and above others? Why are certain kinds of representation 'fashionable' at any given time?

Moral panics and problem youth: the study of media representations from the 1960s to the 1980s

News stories and young people have rarely made happy reading since the advent of print media. As Pearson (1983) has chronicled, the news media have consistently given high profile to the detrimental effects of popular culture on the decline of young people's – and thereby the nation's – moral fibre. Mass media, from their inception, have been closely associated with mass anxiety about young people (Förnas and Bolin 1995). However, the emergence of the notion of 'moral panics' as a way of conceiving of the relationship between the media and young people was to prove an analytical watershed. We shall explore these earlier studies before considering how children and young people are 'repackaged' in contemporary media.

The now famous (or infamous) term 'moral panic' emerged as a key concept in the sociology of deviance in the 1960s, and has since been much appropriated, and some would say, misappropriated, until it has become a part of everyday language. In its original formulation, presented in Stanley Cohen's *Folk Devils and Moral Panics: The Creation of the Mods and Rockers* (1973), 'moral panic' was used to characterize a specific phenomenon in the context of a specific study.

Cohen chronicled a particular set of events – disturbances between groups of youths over a bank holiday weekend in small seaside towns in the south and south-east of England in 1964 – from his own research. He then juxtaposed these alongside the news media's representations of the events. The first point to emerge from this was the discrepancy between the two types of account.

The news media characterized the events in terms of clashes between rival gangs of mods and rockers, seen as scooter and motorbike gangs respectively; the 'gangs' were described as deliberately terrorizing local residents and 'innocent' holidaymakers, as wreaking mass havoc and destruction (particularly arson), causing other serious criminal damage, and carrying out assaults using weapons. The disturbances were presented by the media as being a result of unfettered, undisciplined young people with too much time and money, corrupted by popular music and the values of consumption (see, for example, Abrams 1959).

By contrast, Cohen found that in the original disturbances, the conflicts were largely based on regional rivalries rather than identities of mods and rockers; most of the young people involved were unskilled and semi-skilled workers and not particularly affluent; most did not own scooters or motorbikes; and serious criminal damage and violence were on a considerably smaller scale than the news media claimed. What started out as a fairly modest piece of sociology became obligatory reading in academic circles because of its description of a deviancy amplification spiral which news coverage set in motion. In this process the media characterization of events was seen to arouse public concern on a mass level about the threat of violent young gangs of affluent teenagers threatening the very fabric of society. Not only the misrepresentation of 'facts' is at issue here, but the language and imagery deployed: 'There was Dad asleep in a deckchair and Mum making sandcastles with the children, when the 1964 boys took over the beaches at Margate and Brighton yesterday and smeared the traditional postcard scene with blood and violence' (*Daily Express* 19 May 1964, cited in Cohen 1973: 127).

The public perception thus took hold that the 'mods 'n' rockers' subculture did indeed exist, was growing in strength, and 'something must be done about it'. The result was increased police surveillance and arrests, perceptions by the courts dealing with cases that they were facing a 'new' threat, which then appeared to confirm the 'accuracy' of the initial media prophecies. Along the way this also created an identity which young people in some cases begin to ascribe to themselves, leading to more incidents which would be classed under the same heading, leading to more reaction . . . and so on. Thus a 'moral panic' arises (see Cohen 1973; also many accounts of his work in, for example, Muncie 1984, Förnas and Bolin 1995; Kidd-Hewitt and Osborne 1995; Muncie and McLaughlin 1996).

From Cohen's perspective, then, 'news' representations neither simply reflect reality nor simply invent it, but are produced through a complex set of social relationships between the general public, institutions of social control such as the police and the courts, and young people themselves. Certain groups in society, at certain times, become the scapegoats of wider social pressures. Cohen terms these groups – in this case young people dubbed as mods 'n' rockers – folk devils. This is designed to invoke parallels with the demonization of certain groups and individuals who become symbols of society's ills. Hence, for example:

> For years now we've been leaning over backwards to accommodate the teenagers. Accepting meekly on the radio and television it is THEIR music which monopolizes the air: That in shops it is THEIR fads which will dictate our dress styles . . . we have watched them patiently through the wilder excesses of their ban the bomb marches. Smiled indulgently as they've wrecked our cinemas during their rock and roll films . . . But when they start dragging elderly women around the street . . .
> (*Glasgow Sunday Mail* 24 May 1964, cited in Cohen 1973: 59)

Cohen (p. 60) also reports an inteview by the Margate MP: 'It spreads like a disease. If we want to be able to stop it . . . we must immediately get rid of the bad children so that they cannot infest the good.'

The broader question must then of course be why particular panics arise at particular times, and why certain groups are focused upon as the folk devils of society. This requires us to go somewhat further than Cohen's account, since although Cohen provided some analysis of the deeper social origins of moral panic, he was basing it on one type of case study and was rather more concerned to chart and describe the process than to explain it fully.

Through the 1970s, further key analyses were produced within the 'New Deviancy' tradition (Tierney 1996) which in various ways developed ideas contained within Cohen's work. Young (1974) identified an 'institutionalized need' within the media to create moral panics to 'create good copy' (discussed in Muncie and McLaughlin 1996). Young's by now much-quoted formulation that 'newspapers select events which are atypical, present them in a stereotypical fashion and contrast them against a background of normality which is overtypical' (1974: 241) led to a focus on the structures and interests of news media organizations. Chibnall's (1977) *Law and Order News* went further by producing a typology of the news media's handling of violent crime in the form of 'news values'. The professional cultures of journalists were seen as involving informal 'rules of relevancy', around which 'news values' are built, which in turn influence the selection (of what facts or events to include and exclude) and presentation (the language, imagery, layout, etc.) of news stories. Thus Chibnall's original 'rules of relevancy' highlighted the importance placed by journalists, in the context of violent crime, on visible and spectacular acts, sexual and political connotations, graphic presentation, individual pathology, and deterrence and repression. The main point for the present discussion is that Cohen, Young and Chibnall all produced work which was of crucial importance, both in undermining the notion that the news media reflected reality and in building understandings of the kinds of social imperatives which resulted in the selection of working class young men in particular as the focus of moral panics. These works were subsequently drawn upon in Hall *et al.*'s (1978) *Policing the Crisis*. This, however was a far more wide-ranging work. It is arguably the most significant 'moral panic' analysis of youth, media representation and crime in that it situated the media repackaging of 'youth as problem' firmly within a systematic, complex analysis of representation and the ideological, political and economic structures of a modern society in crisis. We shall consider this in some detail.

Emanating from the Centre for Contemporary Cultural Studies at the University of Birmingham, the authors begin with an account of the way in which the term 'mugging' suddenly, and apparently randomly, emerged in British culture to describe street robbery: a form of crime which has a history spanning centuries. They relate the robbery of an elderly widower by three young men in August 1972 which culminated in the victim being stabbed to death. Based on the phraseology used by a police officer that it was a 'mugging gone wrong', the press precipitated to fame a term which was, in fact, imported from America. However, along with the importation of the term came the importation of its connotations. Britain became seen as under siege from the 'American pattern of urban violence'. Jill Knight, MP, is quoted from the *Birmingham Evening Mail* of 20 March 1973 as saying: 'I have seen what happens in America where muggings are rife . . . It is so absolutely horrifying to know that in all the big American cities, coast to coast, there are areas where people dare not go after dark. I am extremely anxious that such a situation should never come to Britain' (cited in Hall *et al.* 1978: 26).

Hall *et al.*'s point here is that 'mugging' does not simply imply the crime but a whole series of images about the kind of society we are living in, imported from America but applied in the British context (p. 28). Following the initial event (the stabbing), as with Cohen's mods 'n' rockers, both the media and the control agencies seized upon 'mugging' as a new phenomenon. In fact, of course, street robbery had been an endemic aspect of crime in Britain (Pearson 1983). In accordance with Cohen's mode of analysis, Hall *et al.* placed the media account of 'mugging' next to a different kind of account – this time using statistics on street robbery. They concluded that 'mugging was out of all proportion to the actual level of threat', and therefore the moral panic must have arisen out of a perceived or symbolic threat. As with Cohen's study, the media characterization of the phenomenon produced higher levels of public awareness and alarm, and fostered an increasing level of punitive and authoritarian responses from the police and the judiciary, which in turn produced apparently higher levels and seriousness of street crime, which in turn escalated media and public attention . . . Thus far, the argument is familiar. Here, however, Hall *et al.* take a distinctively different turn. While Cohen's account is in some senses compatible with the argument that 'The key role of the media cannot be treated in isolation . . . it can only be analysed together with those other collective agencies in the "mugging" drama – the central control of apparatus in the state: the police and the courts' (Hall *et al.* 1978: 30), *Policing the Crisis* parts company with Cohen's interpretation. It substitutes an account which places the police and the courts, the 'apparatuses' of the state, in a far more crucial position. The strength of the media panic, they argue, could only have had the force it did in a social context of a backlash by an authoritarian state against the liberalizing influences of the 1960s:

> The factor which seems of greatest importance in shaping the 'judicial attitude' in this period is anxiety about growing 'social permissiveness' . . . there was undoubtedly a feeling . . . that the erosion of moral constraints . . . would in the end precipitate a weakening in the authority of the Law itself.
>
> (Hall *et al.* 1978: 34)

In particular, the moral panic surrounding mugging made young black males its 'folk devils', and this again was seen as no accident. Youth, as we have seen, is the recurrent focus of social anxiety in modernity; exacerbated in this case because the 1960s had seen inroads into the liberalization of the juvenile justice system. Thus the Children and Young Persons Act of 1969 proposed to decriminalize juvenile crime almost entirely. That the CYPA was never fully implemented was itself a reflection of the 'moral backlash' which was to characterize the 1970s (see Pitts 1988, 1995, also Chapter 4 in this volume). 'Youth', again, landed squarely in a tussle over the moral fabric of society, with the police, the judiciary, the politicians and the media carving up the delinquent body in their attempts to recoup a perceived loss of authority in the 1960s. The 'new' ingredient, however, was the focus on black youth. Hall *et al.* placed this in the context of heightened racial tension in this period: worsening police–black relations, the growth of Powellism, the growth of the National Front and increasing restrictions on immigration.

However, neither the 'youth' nor the 'black' issues are characterized by the authors simply as a backlash. Rather the backlash was seen to arise from the place of the police and the judiciary as central institutions of the state in a capitalist socio-economic formation experiencing the beginnings of a period of economic instability. The vision of the world presented by Harold Wilson in the early 1960s had been, as Pitts observes (1988: 3), a vision in which the 'white heat of the technological revolution' would 'eradicate poverty and iron out social inequality', and in which, with the expansion of educational opportunity and an enlarged welfare state, full employment would be secured. But by 1970 poverty had been rediscovered, industrial unrest had taken hold as traditional manufacturing industries declined in the international markets, and powerful shop steward actions in the relatively strong motor industries threatened industrial relations. Sterling was weak, inflation was rising, and so was unemployment. A Conservative government was elected under Edward Heath.

It is these developments which Hall *et al.* present as the crucial backdrop to the resurgence of authoritarianism and the scapegoating of black youth, producing, as they did, 'deep structured paradigms about crime in our society', 'English ideologies of crime' (1978: 138) which drew upon the unifying hegemonic ideology of nation. In this context, the moral panic of mugging was able to draw upon the longstanding structures of feeling surrounding youth and nation described in Chapter 1. Once again, young people become the locus of anxiety, this time deflecting attention as the government presided over a crumbling economic infrastructure in which the consensus politics of welfarism were already under threat, if not yet siege.

One need not accept the Marxist analytical framework used in *Policing the Crisis* to appreciate its contribution to an understanding of the framing of 'problem youth'.

Hall *et al.*'s. study expanded the scope of 'moral panic' analysis, not only because it explicitly linked the representation of 'problem youth' to a broader analysis of the social relations of a declining capitalist imperial nation and to the structures of the state, but also because it depicted an important shift in the representation of 'problem youth' more generally. This shift may be characterized as one from 'discrete' moral panics to 'generalized' moral panics. Unlike the specific focus on a single, identifiable 'folk devil', such as the teddy boy, or the mods and rockers, the Hall *et al.* treatment of the mugging panic demonstrated how the image of problem youth was locked by the media into a generalized 'climate of hostility to "marginal" groups and racial minorities' (Muncie 1987; Muncie and McLaughlin 1996).

This elasticity of the concept of moral panic has led to the accusation that it is not a useful concept to characterize the mode of 'repackaging reality', that it 'lacks a precise theoretical grounding' (Muncie 1987). What may rather be the case is that the media representation of 'problem youth', reflecting the uneven processes of historical development, varies historically in its nature and extent. The 1980s, for example, saw a relative diminution in interest in the 'youth problem', with the notable exception of the inner city riots. Even here, despite the politicians' condemnation of young people involved in urban unrest as 'riff raff' spreading a disease of moral degeneration (Beynon and Solomos 1987), and the tabloid press' endorsement of these pronouncements (Beynon and Solomos 1987), the concern at this time was rather with urban disorder and the disenfranchisement of racial minorities in the deteriorating inner cities than with youth per se (unlike the urban disorders of the 1990s, which will be discussed further below). In media portrayals, the 1980s was, to begin with, the era of the 'yuppies' (young urban professionals) benefiting from the temporary monetarist-led property boom originating in the south of England and based on the bubble of financial deregulation. 'Problem youth' remain relatively low profile in the media compared with the images of 'kids in the city', the dog-eat-dog world of the 20-something barrow-boy-turned-share dealer, ambitious young Conservatives hungry for power. This was echoed at the level of popular culture: rather than the cult films of rebellious, anarchistic youth such as depicted in Derek Jarman's epochal film *Jubilee* (1978), we see an emphasis on slick Hollywood productions following the lives of rich college kids or the traumas of urban go-getters such as Jamie (Michael J. Fox) in *Bright Lights, Big City* (1988, based on the 1984 novel by Jay McInerney). If popular imagery were to be believed, rebellion had been replaced by consumption, 'punk' by the 'new romantics'. Was this the death of the moral panic around problem youth?

Not so, however, for seething underneath the veneer of affluence and ambition was a much deeper crisis waiting to happen. By 1982 unemployment had already reached three million – an unprecedented level in the postwar era – and had been increasing dramatically. For, while financial deregulation may have produced an illusion of affluence, the manufacturing infrastructure had of course been rapidly disintegrating. While the yuppies of the south of England babbled hectically into their mobile phones, the tracts of the urban North were populated by young people who were to be the first cohort of post-Beveridge long-term unemployed. Nor were the middle classes exempt: graduate unemployment reached a high in 1982 unrivalled until the 1990s. By the mid-1980s government policy had firmly embraced the rhetoric of the 'skills gap' among our youth; and a 'victim-blaming' culture once again emerged which depicted surging youth unemployment as a crisis 'of' rather than 'for' young people. This was the birth of the 'training scheme' panacea with which the New Right sought to deflect attention from the deep and serious economic decline which had settled in for a long visit. Hence as Griffin (1993) argues, even many academic representations of youth unemployment in the 1980s were marked by a combination of moral panic and paternalistic concern, and constructed mainly through the language of crisis. This reached a crescendo by the middle of the decade . . . much of the debate centred around rising official unemployment levels and speculations about whether youth unemployment represented a cause or a symptom of this 'crisis'.

(Griffin 1993: 67)

At the turn of the decade the British media were once more poised for a fully fledged apoplexy surrounding youth. Something else again, however, was about to happen to the 'moral panic'. The panic was speeding up, and it was spreading. We turn now to examine this transformation in more detail.

A total panic? The media and young people into the 1990s

The history of panic in the 1990s may be characterized less as the 'generalized' panic described by Hall *et al.* (1978) and more as a 'total' panic: a series of discourses of fear reaching out to almost every aspect of the lives of young people, at the same time expanding the catchment age of 'problem youth' downwards to encompass ever younger age groups. There are several distinct 'stories' within this history which it would be wrong to attempt to synthesize overly into a deterministic 'model' of panic. We should be quite clear also that we are in no sense attempting to utilize Cohen's phrase in the sense in which he originally coined it. We continue to use the term 'panic' to suggest the continuity in the demonization of youth under modernism, not to retain its specific sociological application. In suggesting that the 1990s have seen the emergence of a 'total' panic surrounding youth, then, we are seeking to sketch out some general tendencies in the diffusion of fear which may prove to have profound consequences for the understanding of 'youth as problem'.

We begin with a resurgence of the anxiety surrounding youthful consumption of popular culture. Writing of the 'pop chroniclers'' reaction to Acid House music in the late 1980s, Redhead (1990: 1) comments, 'The tale was that Acid House was nothing new; it was merely another, much lauded, link in the subcultural chain, replaying and reworking the 1950s, 1960s, or 1970s.'

Similarly, one might be forgiven for committing the error of thinking that the media reaction to Acid House and the 'summer of love' – encapsulated in headlines such as 'Evil of Ecstasy', 'Ban this killer music', 'Drug crazed Acid House fans', and so on (p. 2) was 'just another moral panic'.

We were about to witness, however, something very different from the earlier representations of problem youth. The first was the creation of a seamless web of anxiety more far-reaching than the long-hair-equals-hippy-equals-psychedelic-drug-taker formula of the late 1960s. A series of overlapping formations surrounding youth consumption and youth behaviour paved the way to the 'post-industrial panic'. Mindless hedonism became portrayed as the new 'culture' of a lost youth. This partly reflected the increasingly intertwining associations of different forms of consumption, each making reference to the other. To begin with there was 'psychedelia, Acid, smiley, beachwear, Lucozade, fluorescent paraphernalia, and so on' (Redhead 1990: 2), and increasingly into the decade, sportswear, football, Britpop, Britlit, Britfrocks, Alcopops . . . Movies of novels, soundtracks of movies, soundtracks of novels, novels of football, music of drugs, novels on drugs . . . and so on. Irvine Welsh catapulted to fame with the hedonist-nihilist novel *Trainspotting*, a novel-on-drugs, followed by the film and the soundtrack, and subsequently by Welsh's rise to further giddy heights as an icon reading to thousands in packed clubland venues.

The youth culture vista is increasingly portrayed as encompassing every feature of consumerism, but without a narrative, without a central theme of conflict, dissent, rebellion or politics. Increasingly, media and political attention turned to the 'problem' of how to regulate a whole, 'lost' generation and a whole field of cultural practice. The 'folk devil' is everywhere young.

Alongside the culture-consumption panic of the 1990s came a resurgence of specific narratives of fear in the form of urban unrest.

The 1990s 'riots' appeared to 'erupt' in Cardiff and Oxford at the beginning of September 1991. In the first case, the trigger appeared to be an attempt by angry crowds to force out a Pakistani shopkeeper after he won a court injunction to stop the shop next door selling bread. The *Wales on Sunday* reported that 'more than one hundred police in riot gear fought to control a mob', and 74 arrests were made (cited in Campbell 1993). In the second case, following police attempts to control 'joyriding' (riding around in stolen cars) and 'hotting' (competitive driving displays in stolen cars) among young men, a cordon was thrown around the area, clashes ensued, and 83 arrests were made (Campbell 1993).

Days later, Dale Robson, aged 17, and Colin Atkins, aged 21, died in a stolen car at the end of a 125 mph police chase on the Meadow Well Estate in Tyne and Wear. The deaths provoked anger among other young people on the estate, some of whom in one notable statement painted: 'POLICE ARE MURDER'S DALE 'N'COLIN WE WONT LET'THEM GET AWAY' (*sic*) on the wall of a community centre. This event, following a build-up of tension in the preceding weeks as police had moved onto the estate to investigate a series of 'ram raids' (a form of burglary on wheels where thieves drive into stores or warehouses through windows or doors), was to form the focus for a media bonanza.

'Violent night shocks "the Bronx"' (*Independent* 11 September 1991) was one headline, apparently referring to a local nickname for the area. The subsequent disturbances – or 'riots' – resulted in the burning out of the community centre, smashing of shop windows, and more arson. Days later, more disturbances took place in the Elswick district, eight miles away. 'Flames of Meadow Well riot spread around the Tyne' declared *The Guardian* (12 September 1991), and 'Youths take to streets in new outbreak of rioting': 'A jeering mob of up to 300 strong set fire to a derelict pub in the Elswick district. Youths performed handbrake turns on cars in front of a crowd outside the blazing building . . . Two fire engines were forced to withdraw after being severely damaged by missiles' (*The Guardian* 12 September 1991).

It was the Newcastle incidents, with their strong visual imagery of macho young men, spectacular displays of stunt driving, burning buildings and rampant lawlessness (even the fire engines were 'stoned'), which were really captured by the media to frame a narrative of despondent, aggressive, lawless young men in a *fin-de-siècle* crisis careering inexorably to the destruction of urban society. Almost any disturbance, small or large, through 1991 to 1993, was to become a 'Meadow Well'-style riot. The regional newspapers, not to be outdone, carved out their share of the 'riot culture'. 'Anarchy on the estates' proclaimed the *Northern Echo* (25 October 1993), providing a map of the North East showing map-pin type fireflashes and with the anarchist logo superimposed. To the right of the graphic, a mini-chronology of 'riot history' in the region is shown, beginning with Meadow Well, and followed by:

28 February 1992: Police stoned by youths in South Shields
27 August 1992: Disturbances on Blue Hall Estate in Stockton
25 May 1993: Youths riot on the Sherburn Estate in South Durham
14 July 1993: Police car stoned on the Edenhill Estate in Peterlee
31 July 1993: Large brawl in Ferryhill market place
4 September 1993: Ragworth Estate sealed off when car is set on fire
24 October 1993: Vandals throw stones at houses and fires started on
   the Skerne Park Estate in Darlington

In true 'moral panic' genre, the application of the term 'riot' extends to cover every incident or disturbance suspected of involving young people. Urgent measures are called for, from policies to tackle unemployment, to more youth clubs, to harsher penalties. Indeed, a twin-track mentality inhabits the media throughout the coverage during this period, simultaneously claiming that starving the estates of money and long-term unemployment produces 'the problem', on the other denouncing the actions of the 'rioters' and calling for harsher penalties and a remoralizing of Britain. What the 'riots' left behind them, however, was a longer lasting media legacy: the spectre of disillusioned urban youth with no foreseeable end beyond the shattering of the social fabric. Visually, the photographs accompanying newspaper articles and the footage on television news on almost any aspect of 'youth' (crime, drugs, alcohol, unemployment . . .) are characterized by tracts of urban wasteland, de-industrialized landscapes, with groups of aimless boys in baggy jeans and hooded tops in the foreground; or run-down council estates, graffiti-ridden, with burned-out cars and again the obligatory aimless boys.

Within these sorry tales of lost generations high on music and drugs or abandoned to mindless urban wrecking, portrayals of macho subcultures rise and bubble for a while: panics within panics. 'Joyriding' took pride of place. The crusading journalist cum self-styled sociologist Bea Campbell clamped the 'macho car culture' on to urban unrest as if it were part and parcel of the same phenomenon (Campbell 1993). 'The macho men who wreck lives' declared Campbell in the *Northern Echo*, referring to her book *Goliath* (1993). In fact, TWOCCing (Taking Without the Owner's Consent) and its predecessor TDA (Taking and Driving Away) have a history as long as the motor car, and TDA is referred to as a popular pastime among the teenage boys in Wilmott's classic *Adolescent Boys in East London* (1966). TDA was still common in the 1970s, and when this author first researched in the North East in 1985, TWOCCing was popular enough to have street 'raps' composed about it. Campbell's inventive if inaccurate 'theorizing' of the youth crime problem provides a typical example of the dangers of creating categories and pouring people into them. In the 1990s, 'joyriding' was to become the symbol of the ultimate destructiveness of dispossessed 'bully' male youth seeking to assert his macho-ness through spectacular posturing in a car he could not afford. This led to wild tales in local, and sometimes national, media reports of children as young as 6 or 7 taking cars.

Our next narrative of panic shows the net of anxiety spreading from youth culture, through car culture, to the mounting wickedness of ever younger children. A 10-year-old Hartlepool boy made national headlines when he 'swaggered free' from court wearing an SAS mask (a balaclava without the hole for the mouth), leading to cries for clampdowns on ever younger criminals. The seamless web grows again, this time with the added horror of children 'as young as 6 or 7' joining in the anarchistic attack on societal values.

And into this scenario came Robbie Thompson and Jon Venables. The facts are now well known: in February 1993 two 10-year-old boys abducted 2-year-old James Bulger from a Liverpool shopping mall, took him on a 2½ mile walk to a railway line, and battered him to death. There was no rational 'motive' available for the killing. On Monday, 1 November 1993, the murder trial began and the politicians and the press immediately made the case stand proxy for all the evils of society on the verge of dystopia. This link is made nicely by David Smith (himself a journalist) in his painstaking chronicle of the 'Bulger case', *The Sleep of Reason* (1994), and is worth quoting at length:

The front page of Thursday's edition of the *Sun* gave a single left hand column to Michael Howard. SUN SPEAKS ITS MIND: YES; CRIME MINISTER . . . 'It was', said the *Sun*, 'a joy to hear a tough talking Home Secretary say he couldn't give a damn if more people ended up behind bars. Never mind three cheers, he deserved one hundred and three for yesterday's declaration of war on the muggers, robbers, and rapists who made our life hell. Bail bandits, young yobs the law couldn't touch, guilty men freed because they stayed silent in court. They were all about to be whacked with a very large stick' . . . The rest of the . . . front page, alongside this column, was consumed by a photograph of Jon, carrying a lollipop, being led in to Preston Crown Court by a policeman with his hand on Jon's shoulder, taken the previous Sunday . . . Page 12 described in spurious detail the boy's luxurious lives in their units as they awaited trial . . . Page 13 was two more photographs (*sic*) . . . One of Bobby, another of Jon, again with their faces obscured. They were, respectively, captioned 'Good Life . . . one of the boys, charged with Jamie's murder . . . has put on weight . . . Sweet treatment . . . the second accused lad clutches a lolly as he is led in to court' . . .

(Smith 1994: 191–2)

Smith argues that the newspaper had waited four days to use these pictures alongside the comment on the Home Secretary's speech. He further notes that throughout the whole trial of the two boys, perhaps '20 minutes out of 17 days, was the full extent of the trial's inquiry into the boys' mental health' (p. 211). In his summing up, the judge told the court, 'It is not for me to pass judgement on their upbringing, but I suspect that exposure to violent video films may in part be an explanation' (p. 227). Smith comments:

It was unclear why the judge had made reference to violent videos. There had been no mention in evidence of any videos. Had he heard the rumours about *Child's Play 3*? . . . If he had wanted to provoke a public debate it was, perhaps, surprising that he had singled out violent videos as a possible explanation for the killing, with no mention of any other issues that might be a factor in young people committing serious crime.

(Smith 1994: 227)

In truth, no one appeared to be concerned with a serious consideration of the aetiology of the crime. Yet of course 'public debate', if it may be graced with the term, certainly ensued: Holland (1997: 49) relates how in the last months of 1993, the face of Chucky Doll, 'a terrifying face, superhuman and unreal, yet freckled and somehow childish', was reproduced over and over again on the front pages of the *Mirror*, the *Sun*, and other newspapers, 'now staring out at a wider public, their millions of readers' (p. 49), until, on 26 November the *Sun* showed the image of Chucky consumed in flames, declaring: 'For the sake of all our kids . . . BURN YOUR VIDEO NASTY.'

Fast-forward now to April 1994: a report is published by Professor Elizabeth Newson, co-signed by 24 child 'experts' comprised of psychologists, psychiatrists and paediatricians. The Newson argument begins with the 'Bulger case'. Thompson and Venables are 'depicted as exemplars of a new cruelty in children . . . something exceptional must explain this new viciousness' (Barker 1997: 15). The Newson report claimed that the ever easier availability of films containing sadistic images in which the viewer is invited to identify with the perpetrator had led to a sea change in violence among children (p. 16). Despite the equal and opposite claims of many other 'experts' and academics, criticizing both the arguments and the evidence of the report, virtually no media attention was paid to dissenting voices. Efforts by the dissenting academics to reach representatives of the major political parties and individual MPs failed, and only the *Times Higher Educational Supplement* published the contrary statement (Barker and Petley 1997: 3). The 'child villain', innocence polluted by video nasties, is here to stay. And not just video nasties: the Newson report makes further links with computers and video games, indeed all forms of 'vicarious viewing'. In their critique of Newson, Barker and Petley point out that the conception of childhood is so 'empty as to be manipulable' (1997: 6; see also Chapter 1 in this volume); they pertinently suggest that 'we need to ask questions about real children as an antidote to these sorts of scare' (p. 6).

A totalizing discourse of panic?

These three 'stories' of end-of-millennium panics raise some unnerving possibilities in the history of 'repackaging problem youth'. Firstly, that the 'discrete' panics surrounding relatively small groups of young people and youth culture have been replaced by a total panic surrounding children and young people. Secondly, that beyond this, we are seeing the birth of a totalizing discourse of panic: a societal anxiety that the last bastions of innocence, purity and hope in society are under siege. If children are not immune, then the implication is that nothing is sacred, and all is corrupted, profaned, in a global web of mass viewing, video nasties, the Internet, popular music. Thirdly, that only a return to ever stronger authoritarianism, censorship, regulation, can save the world 'as we have known it'.

All concern with facts, with balanced debate, is lost in the terror of 'world as horror movie'. In the perception of an inevitable and never ending implosion of morality, the promise of modernity as the harbinger of a better world is submerged under its supposedly self-destructing tendencies. Liberalism is revealed as an illusion, a false promise which is leading to the downfall of civilization.

It is only a logical conclusion that media space is now being given to calls for the introduction of the death penalty for children who kill. Yet young peoples' voices rarely find their way into media discourse; their real lives remain relatively undiscussed. We appear to be far too busy enacting the drama of the millennium tragedy. Were the 'media' a disembedded or dislocated formation, this may not matter, but as we shall see in the following chapter, media representations become ever more closely allied in late modernity with the processes of policy development.

Further reading

Cohen's original *Folk Devils and Moral Panics* (1973) has to be a starting point. Hall *et al.* (1978) should also be looked at. Pearson (1983) again, is interesting and useful. Muncie and McLaughlin (1996: Chapter 1) provide a useful and up-to-date summary of many of the issues touched upon. Barker and Petley (1997), in their edited volume, provide some interesting insights into more recent media panics. Kidd-Hewitt and Osborne (1995) is also of general relevance.

chapter four

_____

In whose interests?
Politics and policy

John Macmillan with Sheila Brown

_____

The languages of youth justice
The advance of welfare: the 1960s
The retreat from welfare: the 1970s
Politicizing criminal justice: the 1980s
Just deserts, false starts: the Criminal Justice Act 1991
Howard's Way
New Labour, new punitiveness?
Politics, policy talk and problem youth
Further reading

Thus far we have dwelt at length on the processes by which youth and crime is constructed through media, politics and academic discourses. Equally important, however, is the question of how policy legislation frames the 'youth crime question' through its *responses* to perceived problems.

In this chapter, we shall examine in detail policy developments between the 1960s and the 1990s, emphasizing that, despite many changes, about-turns and resurrections of old policies under new names, there are underlying themes which dominate the period. We shall see that contemporary policies and practices cannot be understood without a broader historical comprehension of the concerns of commentators, policy-makers and legislators, which in turn relate to the debates and constructions charted in other chapters.

The languages of youth justice

'Youth justice', as a diverse and contradictory policy domain, may be conceptualized at one level as a constellation of languages in which to communicate priorities and practices through which the governance and control of young people is to be achieved. It is important to examine carefully what is being 'said' through policy. This is not a simple matter of semantics, but rather a recognition that all of the words used in framing youth justice carry an array of overt and covert meanings which construct youth and crime in particular ways and which have crucial implications for the lives of young people and the way in which they are positioned within social relations.

Whatever our sources of information – official reports, policy documents, political debate, legislation, the writing of academic commentators or professional practitioners – we find that the discourse surrounding how society should respond to youth crime has been dominated variously by a focus on 'welfare' and/or 'justice', 'care' and/or 'control', 'treatment' and/or 'punishment'. At one level these words provide a useful, if oversimplified, shorthand description of developments which have taken place in youth justice. Thus England and Wales have moved in the last 30 years from a system based on welfare, care and treatment culminating in the Children and Young Persons Act 1969 to a system based on justice, control and punishment following the Criminal Justice Act 1991.

We must include the caveat, however, that these meanings are problematic and not necessarily shared by legislators, policy-makers and professional practitioners. We must therefore approach them critically in terms of both what they 'appear' to say and what they may actually mean. For example, it should be noted that often the concepts are discussed as if they are in opposition: treatment *versus* punishment, welfare *versus* justice (Morris *et al.* 1980). Yet it may also be argued that it is not so much opposition which characterizes these apparently contrasting approaches as the linkages. Hence it may also be claimed that care goes with control (Davies 1986: 69–70), or that 'just welfare' is a viable option (Harris 1985), or that the punishment involved in the deprivation of liberty may be needed for treatment to be effective.

The advance of welfare: the 1960s

Firstly, then, we examine the development of the language of 'welfare' in youth justice, culminating in the Children and Young Persons Act of 1969. How was youth justice framed within the concept of welfare, and what were the implications of such terminology?

There is general agreement that the development of a welfare-based juvenile justice policy culminating in the Children and Young Persons Act 1969 was based on a consensus: the political parties, while they might have differed about the means, accepted the provision of a comprehensive system of state social welfare. We shall not engage in a detailed examination of the legislation prior to 1969 but should note some key developments leading up to the watershed represented by the Children and Young Persons Act 1969 (see Parsloe 1978, Bailey 1987, Harris and Webb 1987, Morris and Giller 1987 for more detailed historical discussion).

There are two important aspects of legislation from the nineteenth century through to the precursor to the 1969 Act: firstly, the development of a range of social control mechanisms specific to young people and, secondly, the widening of the net of social control which affected increasing numbers of working class youth.

Legislative changes in the last half of the nineteenth century extended the scope of summary trial for juveniles under 16, beginning with the Juvenile Offenders Act 1847 (Radzinowicz and Hood 1986: 621–2). The effect of these extensions was 'not simply to transfer to the Petty Sessions those larcenies which had previously been tried at Quarter Sessions . . . but also to increase by a vast extent the number of such larcenies which were tried at all' (Phillips 1977, in Pearson 1983: 216).

Penal developments – Parkhurst as a juvenile prison (1838), the establishment of Reform Schools (1854) and Industrial Schools (1857) – 'saved' children from the adult prison system. At the same time, by separating them, it enabled the authorities to address not just their delinquencies but to seek to re-form their characters and lifestyles within an institutional setting in which rigorous discipline was imposed and which replicated the harsh conditions of industrial employment.

Equally important during this period were the philanthropic and educational initiatives which, while they were directed at 'saving' and 'protecting' children, kept young people off the streets and subjected them to less formal surveillance and controls (see also Chapter 1). As Morris and Giller (1987: 31–2) argue, the objective of these nineteenth-century reforms which began the separation of juvenile from adult offenders were essentially 'authoritarian conservative'. They sought to reaffirm traditional middle class values of family life, parental authority, order and discipline.

The Children Act 1908 represented a major step in the development of the belief that children represented a special category of problem. By establishing Juvenile Courts which were criminal courts in terms of their procedures and giving them jurisdiction over 'care' and 'protection' issues as well as criminal cases, social control was consolidated and extended. In essence the Juvenile Courts became 'family law courts' dispensing family justice (Donzelot 1980: 100). For the first time the courts and the state could intervene directly in working class family life when children were deemed immoral or unruly (Alcock and Harris 1982: 84–5). The conditions which were regarded as indicative of neglect were wide-ranging – including being beyond control, truanting, begging, associating with thieves and prostitutes. Thus the boundaries were blurred between the criminal and the neglected child (Harris and Webb 1987).

In theory, this could have changed in 1927, when the Molony Committee considered substituting civil proceedings for criminal proceedings in the Juvenile Court. Rather than criminalizing neglect, this would have recognized crime as a symptom of neglect, through *decriminalization*. The Committee rejected this option. It was argued that delinquents do commit serious offences, and the public interest requires that they are held responsible for their actions if they are to learn respect for the law (Home Office 1927: 19). However, the Committee also recognized the importance of the welfare of young people who could be the victims of social and psychological conditions and who require individualized 'treatment'. In this respect the Committee felt there was little to distinguish the delinquent from the neglected child. If the offender was to be reformed, full information about his/her home circumstances and schooling was necessary.

The recommendations of the Molony Committee formed the basis of the Children and Young Persons Act 1933. This act is important because it placed a duty on magistrates to consider the welfare of the young person and brought closer together the provisions for the treatment of the delinquent and the neglected. The Act laid down a general principle that, when dealing with offenders and non-offenders, the court 'shall have regard to the welfare of the child or young person and shall in a proper case take steps for removing him from undesirable surroundings and for seeing that proper provision is made for his education and training' (Children and Young Persons Act 1933 Section 44(1)).

The stress on welfare in the CYPA 1933 had two important consequences. Firstly, 'in effect the court became a site for adjudicating on matters of family socialization and parental behaviour even when no 'crime' as such had been committed. When families were 'at fault' the court acted '*in loco parentis*' (Muncie 1984: 45). Secondly, the Molony Committee sought and achieved a widening of the net of social control. 'When it is realised the courts are especially equipped to help rather than punish young people, we hope that the reluctance to bring such people before them will disappear' (Home Office 1927: 23).

Pearson (1983) notes how this perception that Juvenile Courts were places in which young people received 'help' resulted in the number of boys brought before the courts doubling in the three years after the CYPA was implemented. *The Times* commented in 1937 that it was 'not that children have become more wicked . . . but that the legal machinery has become more efficient' (Pearson 1983: 216).

The decade after 1945 has been described as a period of 'penal optimism' (Hood 1974: 376) during which the value of policies which sought to reform and rehabilitate the young offender through individualized 'treatment' was rarely questioned. In 1946 the Curtis Committee (Home Office 1946) reported on the existing modes of provision for children who were deprived of a 'normal' home life. While deprived children were the focus of the Curtis Report, the Committee noted that the difference between such children and delinquents 'is often merely one of accident'. Both were regarded as the victims of family and environmental circumstances which triggered emotional disturbance. Following the report of the Curtis Committee, the Children Act 1948 set up local authority Children's departments to provide, for the first time, a specialized and individualized social work service based on social casework theory to meet the needs of young people. The local authorities '*must* take *into care* any children whose parents did not properly provide for them, or where for some other reason were receiving inadequate care' (Alcock and Harris 1982: 88). The justification for extending the state's right to intervene was the belief that the roots of young people's problems were in the malfunctioning of individuals and their families due to a faulty upbringing.

While the Children Act 1948 addressed welfare issues, seeing young people as victims, the Criminal Justice Act 1948 gave the Juvenile and Magistrates' Court new powers to punish young offenders with the introduction of attendance centres (involving the deprivation of leisure on Saturday afternoons) for those aged 12 to 20 and detention centres (the 'short sharp shock') for those aged 14 to 20. The different approaches adopted in the Children Act and the Criminal Justice Act thus both reflected and strengthened societal ambivalence concerning troublesome youth.

By the 1960s, then, 'welfare' had become the dominant language in relation to juvenile offenders. The Ingleby Committee was set up in 1956 to look into the operation of the Juvenile Court and consider what new powers and duties could be given to local authorities to prevent the neglect of children at home. The report of this committee recognized the inherent conflict when 'justice' and 'welfare' were pursued simultaneously in the same setting. It rightly regarded the Juvenile Court as a criminal court which tried offences employing a 'modified form of criminal procedure', but also acknowledged that

> the requirement to have regard to the welfare of the child, and the various ways in which the court may deal with an offender, suggests a jurisdiction which is not criminal. It is not easy to see how the two principles can be reconciled: criminal responsibility is focused on an allegation about some particular act isolated from the character and needs of the defendant, whereas welfare depends on a complex of personal, family and social considerations.
>
> (Home Office 1960: para. 60)

It is, perhaps, not surprising that a committee largely made up of magistrates, lawyers and administrators but without any social workers, and which accepted the by now commonly held view that the needs of the neglected and the delinquent were the same, with both being a product of family failure, could not resolve this conflict (Bottoms and Stevenson 1992: 34). The solution proposed was to retain the Juvenile Court because the available disposals interfered with a young person's liberty, but to raise the age of criminal responsibility from 8 to 12 (and eventually 14), with care and protection proceedings replacing criminal proceedings. It was thought by maximizing 'welfare' considerations for children under 14 more would be referred to the court. As Morris and Giller (1987: 76–7) note, the report endorsed a social welfare approach but the reforms addressed only procedural issues.

Bottoms (1974) points out that the report was received coolly by the Conservative government, which was concerned about the increase in juvenile crime. The age of criminal responsibility was raised by the Children and Young Persons Act 1963 to 10 with little enthusiasm – the House of Lords voted for 12. Although the CYPA 1963 was a limited measure it did give local authorities the duty to engage in preventative work with children and families thought to be 'at risk'. Whereas the Children Act 1948 had given social workers the task of rescuing children by taking them into care, the CYPA 1963 sought to prevent 'trouble' before it developed.

The consequence of this shift from reactive to proactive social work was far-reaching. Child care officers and family caseworkers were given a mandate to search for social problems in poor families, and not surprisingly they found them, 'armed' with their 'bible' – Bowlby's (1951) *Maternal Care and Mental Health*, which purported to show that short- and long-term maternal deprivation led to the development of maladjusted and delinquent personalities. Delinquent children and deprived children were seen as the products of – victims of – undesirable family and social circumstances. Nineteenth-century beliefs about the moral deficiencies of working class family life, lack of parental care and discipline had, by the middle of the twentieth century, been given a scientific gloss. Thus a strategy designed to reduce the number of children coming into care ended up sucking in a new population of children 'at risk' into the increasingly welfare-oriented juvenile justice system. The problem of delinquency had become synonymous with the 'problem family' (Clarke 1980); but, unlike the nineteenth century, when the immorality of working class family life was the object of attention, it was now those families who had fallen through the net of postwar reconstruction, the 'residue', or 'residual problem' of delinquency linked to poverty.

Thus, as with our discussion in Chapter 2, we need to appreciate the social and political context of postwar optimism.

The report of the Longford Study Group in 1966 (a private Labour party committee on which professional social work was not represented), whose proposals were embodied in the 1965 White Paper *The Child, the Family, and the Young Offender* (Home Office 1965), regarded minor offending as 'part of the normal process of growing up' (Clarke 1980: 85). Generally, more serious offenders were 'the victims of a deprived and unhappy home' (Harwin 1982). As 'victims' they should not be held criminally responsible for their actions. Thus the 1965 White Paper proposed non-judicial Family Councils in place of the Juvenile Courts for young people under 16, staffed by social workers and involving parents in discussions: the welfare needs of the child and the family would become central to the whole process (Harwin 1982). Councils would be able to order the child (parents) to pay compensation, arrange supervision by social workers and utilize local authority residential institutions. The age of criminal responsibility would be raised to 16, and those aged 16–20 would be dealt with in Young Offender Courts, which would be concerned with the welfare of the offender as well as with punishment.

If these proposals had been adopted, juvenile offending would have been effectively decriminalized. However, they were extensively criticized by powerful groups with a vested interest in the juvenile justice system (Bottoms 1974; Harwin 1982). Lawyers objected to the due process of the law being replaced by administrative procedures lacking legal safeguards. Clerks to the Justices and Magistrates saw their role disappearing, and argued that the proposals would fail to protect the public adequately. The Probation Service felt threatened by the prospective loss of their responsibility for supervising young offenders at a time when the future of the service was in doubt. It was argued that the authority of the court was necessary to deal with 'difficult or inadequate offenders' (Harwin 1982). Finally, the White Paper was opposed by the Conservatives, and the Labour government had a majority of only three (Bottoms 1974), and the Labour party's own Home Secretary, Roy Jenkins, was unsympathetic, as were Home Office civil servants. The proposals foundered on the strength of the opposition.

By contrast, Bottoms (1974) argues that the 1968 White Paper *Children in Trouble* (Home Office 1968) succeeded where the earlier White Paper had failed because it retained the Juvenile Court, and thereby defused the objections (in the short term at least) of lawyers, magistrates and probation workers. At the same time, social work as a profession was gaining in strength, and the emergence in the top echelon of the Home Office of civil servants with a strong child care orientation was significant. The result was the Children and Young Persons Act of 1969, underpinned by a philosophy of treatment which removed any lingering distinction between children who offended and those who needed 'care and protection': the causes of delinquency and deprivation were seen as the same; both kinds of children suffered from essentially the same problems and had the same 'treatment' needs. Primacy is given to the family and the social circumstances of the deprived and underprivileged whose circumstances caused crime, truancy, lack of control and neglect – but it should be noted that primacy was accorded to individual factors, rather than structural factors such as poverty or poor housing. Thus Morgan (1981: 47) has argued that 'As "need" replaced neglect, the welfare targets of the Act were subtly shifted from differences in people's life chances to the deficiencies in their personalities and the mess they were making in their interpersonal relationships.'

Moreover, because the White Paper claimed that delinquency was 'often' a part of the normal growing-up process, but 'sometimes' a 'symptom of a deviant, damaged, or abnormal personality', observation, assessment and flexible 'treatment' were required.

The CYPA of 1969 was, then, a watershed in the development of a welfare approach: it represented a culmination of the preceding developments of the twentieth century. However, it is important to recognize that the rationale of the Act was based on care and control. Thus the Home Secretary, James Callaghan, claimed 'there is general agreement that care and control run in harness' (cited in Davies 1986: 70). Hence as Davies comments, care and control are seen as 'mutually supportive, complementary, and even synonomous. Coercive and restrictive forms of containment and restriction were justified as "good for the child" and meeting his or her "needs"' (Davies 1986: 69).

So, while one may be lulled by the language of welfare into thinking that the shift from 'punishment' to 'welfare' in the Act was progressive, it actually represented a further erosion of children's rights, as it left social workers to determine the 'best interests' of the child or young person. Indeed, the whole language – and practice – of welfare becomes problematic on closer inspection. The meaning of 'care', 'needs', 'best interests', 'good for the child', cannot be taken at face value. As Allen has argued,

> If the measures result in the compulsory loss of the child's liberty, the involuntary separation of the child from his [sic] family, or even the supervision of a child's activities by a probation worker, the impact on the affected individuals is essentially a punitive one. Good intentions and a flexible vocabulary do not alter this reality
>
> (Allen 1964, cited in Morris 1978: 58)

The *reality* of care, then, often does not mean what we would commonly assume from the connotations of the word; it can also mean 'locking up into care', 'taking into care', the granting of legal permission to social workers to remove a child from the home and place him or her into an institution (Cohen 1985: 277) – where, as we shall see in Chapter 5, she or he may be vulnerable to further layers of victimization through physical or sexual abuse.

The Children and Young Persons Bill was debated in Parliament at (yet another) time of anxiety about increasing juvenile crime. The debate in fact focused less on the overall 'welfare' objective of the Bill than on the means to appease this anxiety. Davies (1986: 74–6) argues that the desirability of 'welfare' measures may have been seen as valid by academics and social work professionals, but it lacked 'deep popular roots'. It was never accepted by organized Labour or working class voters. The Labour government therefore stressed that it was not 'soft' on punishment, since care and control went together. The government conceded that custodial institutions would need to remain in place for juveniles until 'alternative provision' became available. Meanwhile, the Conservative party opposed the reduced role of the courts. Politically speaking, one weakness of the Bill was that unlike previous reforms, it actually threatened the existing institutions and legal procedures (Bailey 1987). Thus when the Conservative party won the general election in 1970, they would not implement central clauses of the Act.

The retreat from welfare: the 1970s

Since the language of welfare was ambiguous, since in its purist form it did not have support from powerful sectors, and since in any case it was grafted onto, rather than fundamentally challenging, an existing criminal justice system, it was a simple matter for the Conservative government to undermine it. The police and the magistrates retained many of their powers, the age of criminal responsibility was maintained at 10, and attendance centres, detention centres and borstals for juveniles were to be phased out only if social services developed 'suitable alternatives'. The retreat from welfare had begun before it had arrived. Even those portions of the CYPA (1969) which were retained were soon attacked vociferously by police and magistrates, who argued that it left them powerless to deal adequately with juvenile offenders. Again, it must be remembered that these changes took place within the postwar concern with increasing crime rates in the face of affluence. The police and the magistracy were able to play on the perception that delinquents were increasingly roaming the streets, running wild and offending with impunity.

It is important to note here that such perceptions were largely false. Firstly, Pearson (1983: 217) points out that the apparent 'crime wave' in the 1970s was 'totally fictitious'. It resulted, he argues, almost entirely from a change in police practices. The use of the formal caution (which was recorded) increased, replacing the informal warnings before 1969 (which were not recorded). Superficially, the diversion from the criminal justice system envisaged by the CYPA seemed to have occurred. However, research indicates that any diversion which was achieved was very limited (Ditchfield 1976; Bottomley and Pease 1986: 119–22). In reality, yet again, as following the legislation in 1908, 1933 and 1963, a 'welfare' measure had widened the net of social control to register more children and young people as delinquent. The consequence was an inflation in the level of recorded crime which stimulated yet another moral panic about youth crime. Since despite magistrates' protestations, the only partial implementation of the 1969 Act had left them with direct access to custodial sentencing for juveniles, the use of these sentences and of the attendance centre escalated during the 1970s. In contrast the use of care orders and supervision orders declined. During the 1970s the courts were using custody more frequently, earlier in young people's criminal 'careers', and for less serious offences (Millham *et al.* 1978).

The persistence of the belief in the 1970s 'crime wave' stemmed partly from the power of the Justice's Clerk's Society, the Magistrates' Association and the Police Federation, with their access to governmental sources; it also continued because the views of these bodies coincided with the Conservative government's expressed doubts about the CYPA within the context of their developing platform of 'fighting crime', restoring social discipline and asserting the ideology of 'individual responsibility' (Pitts 1988: 28).

Meanwhile, there were a range of 'problems' in relation to the social work profession in the 1970s which according to Harwin (1982) combined to call into question the value of social work treatment of delinquents. The Home Office Children's Department (which had drafted the 1969 CYPA) was abolished at the same time that social work was reorganized with the establishment of generic social services departments without adequate resources; few social workers had experience in dealing with 'difficult' young offenders; social work practice was oriented towards casework with individuals and found it hard to come to terms with the unfamiliar controlling demands of their role; social workers themselves failed to develop effective community-based programmes as alternatives to custodial punishment. In such a climate, dramatic events such as the failure of social workers to prevent the battering to death of a child (Maria Colwell, known to be at risk), facilitated further erosion of the credibility of social work. As with the responses to the James Bulger case 20 years later,

> reforms of the system take place not so much because of a careful routine analysis by ministers and civil servants . . . nor even because of a critique or exposé by an outside journalist or pressure group, but because one or more individual incidents occurs, drawing attention to some underlying imperfections of policy in a dramatic way which seems to demand change.
>
> (Bottoms and Stevenson 1992: 23)

The tenacity of the magistrates and the Police Federation, and the inability of social workers to respond to concerns about their ability to cope with offenders, meant that when the Labour government elected in October 1974 reviewed the operation of the CYPA, it did not consider that the full implementation of the Act would solve the problems associated with it. The House of Commons Expenditure Committee in 1975 concluded that 'The major failing of the Act is that it is not wholly effective in differentiating between children who need care, welfare, better education and more support, from the small minority who need strict control and an element of punishment' (1975: para. 167).

The Committee's view reflected the changed nature of the debate about how to deal with juvenile offenders. 'Ordinary' delinquents were not an issue; concern focused on the 'hard core of criminals for the future who required stronger punitive measures' (Scotland Yard statement 1 July 1974, in *The Guardian* 2 July 1974). The Expenditure Committee's solution was a twin track, 'bifurcatory' approach which distinguished the less serious occasional offenders from the more serious persistent offenders. Morris and Giller's interpretation was that the Committee was influenced more by 'an image of a physically mature, often economically independent, adolescent who was a threat to the established order' than by 'an image of the juvenile in trouble or need of care' (1987: 109). It is this perceived 'hard core' of serious and/or persistent offenders which continued to excite politicians, policy-makers and practitioners through the 1980s to the present time. Whereas the 1969 CYPA had been predicated on the similarities of care and control cases, in the 1970s the differences were being highlighted.

Although a White Paper in 1976 on the CYPA reaffirmed the philosophy of the 1969 Act (Home Office 1976) in accepting the value of non-residential care or supervision and intermediate treatment for the majority of 'soft end' offenders, it supported firmer measures for 'hard end' offenders through the use of attendance centres and detention centres (Morris and Giller 1987: 111). In addition, financial assistance was to be provided to local authorities to expand residential accommodation and places in youth treatment centres for the most 'disturbed' young offenders. As Harwin (1982) points out, the government did not seek to alter the balance of power in the courts between the magistrates and social workers, but sought instead to give added 'control' responsibilities to social workers for persistent offenders by banning the courts from remanding 14-year-olds into custody and encouraging the building of secure accommodation. Concurrently came an increased emphasis on the use of more intensive forms of intermediate treatment (IT) concentrating on behaviour modification rather than a needs-based model, which had been the intention of the original IT (Pitts 1988: 37–9).

These changes occurred in a wider context of general disillusionment with 'treatment' among academics and civil liberties organizations. The 'collapse of the rehabilitative ideal' (Cavadino and Dignan 1997) was imminent. Reviews of the literature on attempts to rehabilitate and treat offenders inside and outside institutions suggested 'nothing works' (for example, see Lipton *et al.* 1975 and Brody 1976). The dominant 'medical model' was accused of being 'theoretically faulty'; more specifically, social workers were criticized for the subjectivity of their judgements, for the seemingly discriminatory way in which they exercised their discretion, and for their willingness to use institutional care and recommend custody in their reports to the courts. Young people were being deprived of their liberty and parents of their 'rights' without adequate legal controls (Bean 1976; Taylor *et al.* 1979; Morris *et al.* 1980; Thorpe *et al.* 1980).

Politicizing criminal justice: the 1980s

By 1979 Britain was in the throes of an economic crisis, the 'mugging' scare had commandeered the headlines (see Chapter 3), and industrial unrest was out of control. Anxiety was rampant. The Conservative election campaign 'made more of law and order, in a more strident and populist way, than hitherto' (Windlesham 1993: 144).

King (1991) sees the crime problem at this time as constructed to fit the particular ideological vision of society held by the political party in power, so that the 'identification of causes' and the solutions adopted becomes a 'political rather than a rational scientific exercise' (King 1991: 87). During the 1980s the government consistently emphasized the importance of individual responsibility, initiative and self-discipline within the context of a free market economy as the only way of achieving the 'good life' (p. 94). As Brake and Hale (1992: 2–3) argue, 'The conservative government was setting its agenda around law and order, welfare, shiftlessness, and immorality. It intended to move social responsibility back to the individual and morality back to the family.'

Any link between social conditions and crime had to be rejected because such a link would have implied increased public expenditure involving welfare benefits, which the government was pledged to reduce.

Law and order rhetoric portrayed offenders as 'evil people', as fundamentally different from law abiding citizens. King (1991: 91) notes some of the epithets used to describe youth offenders by Tory politicians and the tabloid press: louts, thugs, brutes, hooligans and monsters, all surfaced or resurfaced. Delinquents were no longer social casualties. They were deliberate lawbreakers who must be held responsible for their actions – in other words, they were young criminals. Insofar as offending had a cause, its roots lay in a decline in discipline and a growth in permissiveness in families and schools. This produced a lack of respect for adults, authority and the law. Crime could only be controlled if it was punished more severely by tougher custodial and non-custodial sentences. The police needed to be strengthened and the courts given increased powers. Thus the attendance centre order was promoted and the provision expanded as 'a disciplinary method of invading the leisure time of hooligans and vandals', and the regime of the detention centres was modelled on army 'glass houses' 'as a short sharp shock to violent young thugs' (Windlesham 1993: 152). Windlesham (p. 157–60) makes clear that the changes in the detention centre regimes were implemented against Home Office advice and despite the opposition of the Prison Service and penal reform groups.

In developing criminal justice and youth policies consistent with their political philosophy, the Conservative government immediately axed the non-political Advisory Council on the Penal System which had been used by previous Labour and Conservative governments as an aid to policy formulation. It disappeared not because it was ineffective but because 'of the Government's distaste for independent advice', according to Louis Blom-Cooper in a letter to *The Times* (29 August 1981, cited in Windlesham 1993: 150).

In 1980, a White Paper on 'young offenders' (Home Office 1980) was published which indicated clearly government thinking in dealing with offenders under the age of 21. It shifted the emphasis from the 'child in need' to the 'juvenile criminal' (Morris and Giller 1987: 119). The approach proposed was to be refined and developed through the 1980s, culminating in the Criminal Justice Act 1991. The 1980 White Paper advocated diversion from the court through the expansion of cautioning for minor offenders, which it claimed would reduce reoffending (Home Office 1980: para. 38); but also proposed tougher penalties for serious offenders, including more demanding forms of non-custodial supervision.

The Criminal Justice Act 1982, which incorporated most of the proposals in the White Paper, 'represented a move away from treatment and lack of personal responsibility to notions of punishment and individual and parental responsibility' (Gelsthorpe and Morris 1994: 972). While allowing individual 'treatment' to be pursued in relation to the supervision order and the probation order, the Home Secretary stressed the retributive model of making the punishment fit the crime (Windlesham 1993: 165).

The CJA 1982 was important because it accorded magistrates increased powers to determine the form and content of Juvenile Court disposals through the attachment of conditions to supervision orders and the extension of community service orders to juveniles, thus demonstrating a further rejection of social work; it simultaneously required social workers to exercise more control and discipline when supervising juvenile offenders. For the first time, however, courts were restricted in their use of custody for offenders below the age of 21. These restrictions were not part of the original Criminal Justice Bill, but resulted from amendments proposed by members of the Parliamentary All Party Penal Affairs Group which were actually opposed by the government (Windlesham 1993: 167–9).

Morris and Giller (1987: 132–3) see the policy changes introduced by the CJA 1982 as largely political and ideological in that the measures introduced were not based on research. For the government they had symbolic value in that 'they provided the appearance of a strong government willing to take tough measures against crime' (p. 133). This interpretation is supported in the history of the detention centre. In 1985, Home Secretary Leon Brittan extended the 'experiment' of short sharp shock regimes in some detention centres to all such institutions (Home Office 1984). Hence 'it is hard to avoid the conclusion that sound penal administration had been made to serve the needs of a defective icon of political ideology' (Windlesham 1993: 161).

Despite the government's belief in the value of the punitive detention centre, pragmatism triumphed over symbolism, and their actual use by magistrates declined. This, however, was compensated for by an increased use of youth custody, rooted partly in magisterial belief that these offered 'training' and were therefore more constructive. Consequently the 1988 Criminal Justice Act replaced the separate detention centre and youth custody sentences with a single sentence of detention in a young offender institution. This Act also allowed courts to attach a new condition to supervision orders that the offender comply with local authority education requirements; this in effect criminalized non-school attendance.

It should be noted here that the 1980s saw a sharp fall in the use of custodial sentences for juveniles, due mainly to the restrictions on custody included in the CJA 1982 and the CJA 1988. However, an increased use of 'punitive' community measures occurred in this period, particularly intensive intermediate treatment (IIT) orders. Fifteen million pounds were made available following the 1982 Act to voluntary organizations for the development of IIT schemes. These were to be offence-focused as alternatives to custody, and were supported by the government ideologically insofar as they would control and discipline young offenders. The money was not offered to social services departments, thus completing the refashioning of intermediate treatment in a 'law and order' image (Cohen 1985: 139–55; Davies 1986: 83–4). The projects were managed on an inter-agency basis, including social workers but also probation, voluntary organizations, the police and Juvenile Court magistrates, further linking them into a criminal justice structure.

In 1981, the Parliamentary All Party Penal Affairs Group had proposed statutory criteria to restrict the use of custody and care, and had recommended the increased use of non-custodial sentences and the extension of cautioning. Successive Home Office Circulars in 1985 (14/1995) and 1990 (59/1990) used increasingly strong language to encourage the use of the formal caution with prosecution as a last resort, and advocating the use of post-cautioning 'support services' when 'problems' or 'needs' were identified. The result was a massive increase in cautioning. The growth of inter-agency panels and juvenile liaison bureaux required police and social services to work together, thus shifting the police into 'areas of social intervention previously guided by social workers' assessment of the needs of the child and the family' (King 1991: 103). Conversely, the social work agencies were shifted into an area of decision making previously reserved for the police – the decision to prosecute.

This discussion of legislative and policy developments in juvenile justice in the 1980s has shown an increase in the proportion of juveniles cautioned and a decrease in the numbers sentenced to custody. How does this fit with the ideology of a government apparently committed to a more authoritarian solution to social problems (Hall *et al.* 1978) and a more repressive juvenile justice system (Clarke 1985)? Pratt (1990), in his analysis of the form and nature of social control, draws attention to the pragmatic approach adopted by the Conservative government and their concern with efficiency and cost effectiveness in the management of recalcitrant youth. This involves dealing differently with the minor/occasional offender and the serious/persistent offender: a policy of bifurcation. Prosecution is costly and the juvenile justice system unpredictable. Magistrates may decide on a discharge but they may opt, unnecessarily, for some form of supervision. If many young people do not reoffend after a formal caution, why prosecute them? If they can be persuaded to accept some form of voluntary supervision, activity or reparation, then they can be brought under control and subjected to surveillance more cheaply and efficiently than by processing them through the courts. Custody is extremely costly and reconviction rates are very high, so that the pragmatic logic would be to restrict the use of custody to a minority of 'hard core' offenders requiring punishment. Most non-custodial sentences can be 'strengthened' to provide control and discipline at less cost. The ideological focus by the government on law and order must be balanced against its ideological commitment to anti-welfarism and decreased public spending, thus helping to explain the apparently perplexing juxtaposition of the 'darkest hour' for juvenile justice with some of the greatest successes in reducing custodial sentencing through 'systems management', developed by juvenile justice agencies working together at the local level and not directly seeking to change government policy (Cavadino and Dignan 1997).

Also, the changes in juvenile justice needs to be placed in the context of wider economic, social and policy developments which have increased significantly the state's surveillance and regulation of youth. Davies (1986: 81–2) draws attention to the inner city riots of 1981 and 1985, incidents of violence at football matches, and the miners' strike of 1985. These events strongly influenced ministers and were taken as evidence both of a breakdown in social discipline and the need to combat lawless behaviour, if not particularly youth lawlessness. The Police and Criminal Evidence Act 1984 strengthened police powers of stop and search, and the Public Order Act 1985 gave the police considerable discretion in dealing with disorderly behaviour; both heightened the climate of intolerance and could be used in practice to increase the surveillance and control of the young even if that had not been their original intention.

Most IIT in the late 1970s and early 1980s was preventative in that it involved those perceived to be at risk of offending – non-school attenders, disruptive pupils, unemployed youth. Pratt (1983) sees this form of social intervention as a means of regulating and 'normalizing' unattached and potentially threatening youth. Similarly, Bottoms and Pratt (1989) suggest that developments in IIT for girls in the 1980s seemed designed to produce 'normal' girls. Furthermore, ministers, the Home Office and the police promoted an expansion of the 'preventative' role of the police in schools and youth work, including organizing sporting and leisure activities for disadvantaged young people (King 1991: 103–4). These activities gave the police a more direct involvement in young people's lives and moved them into the field of social work.

Carlen (1996) shows how welfare policies in the 1980s shifted from what she describes as 'facilitative disciplinary welfare' to 'repressive disciplinary welfare' (Carlen 1996: 29–30): 'the overall outcome of welfare, housing, educational, training, and employment policies during the 1980s resulted in a much strengthened disciplining of pauperised and redundant youth *independent of the criminal justice and/or penal system*' (pp. 45–6, original emphasis).

These policies treated youth as a 'dangerous class' to be denied adult status and the rights and duties of citizenship. The government refused to recognize that young people had 'needs' independently of their families and sought to 'enforce their continuing dependence on adults, especially parents' (Davies 1986: 127) as a means of controlling them.

Just deserts, false starts: the Criminal Justice Act 1991

The years 1987 to 1991 were to prove a period of intense activity and significant changes in the field of criminal justice policy. It was a brief interlude during which policy-making was characterized more by principle than by an ad hoc response to the political and pragmatic exigencies of the moment. This brief flowering of relative rationality, probably engineered through an alliance between Douglas Hurd (Home Secretary 1985–9) and David Faulkner (Under Secretary of State in charge of the Home Office Research and Statistics Division 1982–90), arose from a cautious and reasoned approach to policy-making rarely seen in criminal justice (Windlesham 1993 and Rutherford 1996 comment in more detail on this alliance).

Hurd articulated a consistent message based on 'just deserts'. He envisaged a 'wider and tougher range of community based sentences' in his speech to the Conservative Party Conference in 1989 (Rutherford 1996: 104) which, he argued, would be potentially more effective 'than the often pointless, and sometimes corrupting, experience of imprisonment' (Windle-sham 1993: 462). Again, of course, reductions in public expenditure (particularly the soaring costs of prison building) may be seen by the cynical as an issue here.

Between 1987 and the publication of the White Paper *Crime, Justice, and Protecting the Public* (Home Office 1990), considerable efforts were made by the Home Office and ministers to gain the support of the criminal justice agencies for the proposed reforms. A major political problem even at this stage was that the eventual triumph of the law and order ideologies of the post-1979 period had fostered expectations of harsher punishment and damaged the credibility of non-custodial penalties. The Conservative party needed to be won over to an ideologically unpalatable change in policy, the judiciary to sentencing reforms which would limit sentencers' discretion and the probation service to punishment in the community (Windlesham 1993). Windlesham (p. 245) describes the White Paper as 'a classic statement of public policy'. It sought to establish the objectives of the criminal justice system and provide a framework for sentencing offenders of all ages. Sentencing should be 'based on the seriousness of the offence or just deserts' (para. 2.3), and be 'in proportion to the seriousness of the crime' (para. 2.2), although 'depending upon the offence and the offender, the sentence may also aim to achieve public protection, reparation, and reform of the offender, preferably in the community' (para. 2.9). Deterrence was rejected because 'it is unrealistic to construct sentencing arrangements on the assumption that most offenders will weigh up the possibilities in advance and base their conduct on rational calculation. Often they do not' (para. 2.8).

The White Paper adopted a 'twin track' or 'bifurcatory' approach to sentencing which distinguished between property offenders (excluding domestic burglary) and those convicted of violent or sexual offences. The former were envisaged as being normally dealt with in the community, or by shortened prison sentences. The latter were seen as requiring custody and longer sentences. Punishment should be based on the restriction of liberty 'applied either in the community or through custodial penalties' (para. 2.11), but 'nobody now regards imprisonment, in itself, as an effective means of reform for most prisoners . . . it can be an expensive way of making bad people worse' (para. 2.7), and 'more offenders should be punished in the community' (para. 4.1).

There are serious flaws with a 'just deserts' philosophy. It oversimplifies the relationship between crime and its punishment. By making the criminal act the criterion for punishment it rules out of consideration the 'material realities' of offenders' lives (Davies 1986: 87), creating a structure of punishment but saying nothing of the causes of crime. Despite the coercive and covertly punitive potential of the 'welfare' approach discussed earlier in this chapter, it did involve a concern for the needs of the deprived and disadvantaged. The White Paper further distanced itself from such an approach in its specific provisions for young people, replacing the Juvenile Court by the 'Youth Court' dealing with a wider age range of 10–17 years, and emphasizing that young people aged 16 and 17 'should be dealt with as near adults' (para. 8.16). Since 'care' cases had already been removed from the Juvenile Court under the 1989 Children Act, 'welfare' was by now on the distant horizon. The focus on the family as the 'site' of youth crime was retained as central, but with an eye to parental discipline and control rather than deprivation, making provision for courts to require the attendance of parents, to order parents to pay financial penalties, or to bind over parents of young people convicted of criminal offences (paras. 8.7 and 8.8). Moreover, offence-focused pre-sentence reports (PSRs) replaced the welfare-focused social inquiry reports (SIRs). Although report writers were still required to address 'welfare' issues, this would seem to be little more than a gesture (given the strong emphasis on the seriousness of the offence); in practice this would probably amount more to a mitigation plea than a true consideration of 'needs'.

Despite the focus on just deserts and the distantiation from 'welfare', the proposals had already run into trouble by the time the Criminal Justice Bill was published (nine months after the White Paper). The most punitive aspects of the legislation were being emphasized. The new Home Secretary, David Waddington, argued that the Bill was not designed to reduce the prison population, thus contradicting the White Paper; he also emphasized lengthy imprisonment for violent and sexual offenders, and toughened-up community punishments. This, unsurprisingly, has been related to political fears that conservative opinion might turn against the Bill, seeing the more controlled use of custody and the emphasis on community punishment as 'soft options'. Meanwhile, the changes proposed by the Criminal Justice Act 1991 necessitated extensive preparation and training of criminal justice personnel, and implementation was delayed until October 1992. The intervening period was to assure the demise of the rational aspects of the White Paper.

Howard's Way

By 1991 'crime pressure' (Radzinowicz, cited in Rutherford 1996: 14) had mounted and the stage was once more set for a return to 'short cut solutions', the hallmark of 'authoritarian systems of government' (p. 14). After the brief respite of policy at least based on reasoned argument, a new era of authoritarian and punitive penal populism was born, in the 'form of campaigns against "bail bandits" and "joyriding"' (Newburn 1995: 121), which were the subject of intense media attention. The police responded by 'cracking down' on public displays of joyriding, and there were serious confrontations with young men which led to disturbances on housing estates in the form of the 1990s 'riots' (see Chapter 3). The government responded by speedily enacting a new offence of Aggravated Vehicle Taking with a maximum penalty of five years imprisonment. The courts responded by treating this offence as on a par with domestic burglary and 'deserving' a custodial sentence. At the same time, Kenneth Baker, now Home Secretary, blamed the parents and sought to establish a 'clear relationship between problem families, delinquent youth, and the (re)production of a criminal underclass' (McLaughlin and Muncie 1993: 155).

When Kenneth Clarke became Home Secretary in April 1992 after the general election, he gave the impression that he was 'unhappy not only with the CJA 1991 but with the generally liberal course that had been pursued in the latter part of the 'eighties' (Rutherford 1996: 127). Rutherford also argues that Clarke had an eye to the danger of Tony Blair stealing 'his party's law and order mantle' (pp. 127–8), with his rhetoric of 'tough on crime, tough on the causes of crime'. The CJA 1991 was undermined within a few months of its implementation in October 1992. It was criticized as restrictive by the Lord Chief Justice and the Magistrates' Association: government response was swift. The Criminal Justice Act 1993 'amended' the 1991 Act, most notably loosening the criteria governing custodial sentences. Custody had returned to the forefront of the political agenda in a political climate eloquently expressed by John Major, the Prime Minister: 'society needs to condemn a little more and understand a little less' (*Mail on Sunday* 21 February 1993).

Meanwhile during 1991 the police had initiated a 'sophisticated campaign . . . converted into a moral panic by the media' (Rutherford 1996: 127) which focused on a small number of persistent offenders. The offenders were said to be responsible for a disproportionate amount of crime in the areas in which they lived, and neither the police nor the courts had the powers to deal with them (Hagell and Newburn 1994: 19–22). Early in 1993 when the House of Commons Home Affairs Commission examined the issue it was presented with conflicting evidence – of a rise in juvenile crime (Association of Chief Police Officers) and a reduction in juvenile crime (Home Office) – which it was unable to resolve. Indeed, the Justices' Clerks' Society questioned the 'concept of the persistent offender' and the 'danger of emotive reactions . . . resulting in "sentence by label"' (Gibson *et al.* 1994).

Kenneth Clarke had already indicated his willingness to introduce secure training orders for 12- to 14-year-olds to combat the 'problem'.

By the time Michael Howard became Home Secretary in 1993, the 'folk devilling of children and young people' (Carlen 1996: 48), escalating since 1991, had gathered force as 'the Bulger case' provided a window into the worst imagined excesses of youth crime (see Chapters 1 and 3). At the Conservative Party Conference in October 1993 Howard outlined a wide range of 'tough' policies to cut crime which would increase the use of custodial sentences and which he justified by claiming 'prison works'.

Some aspects of the role of the tabloid press in this context have been explored in Chapter 3; suffice it to note that Jonathan Steele, writing in *The Guardian* (7 March 1997), commented:

> Howard's appointment as Home Secretary coincided with a surge of interest in the tabloid and the Murdoch press. Lord Windlesham, a former Tory Home Office Minister who made a study of crime stories, found *The Times* running 10 a day in August 1993, while the *Sun* ran a 'campaign for justice', highlighting violent crime. 'Howard's strategy could not have been more different from his predecessor's', says Windlesham. 'He [Howard] was generally dismissive of professional expertise, including at times advice from his own officials. Before long a consistent pattern could be detected of conforming to perceived public opinion, taking particular notice of the coverage of crime and editorial comment in the press'.

Thus it seems that advice, unless it was the media's 'advice', was to be ignored. What seemed rhetoric was to become policy.

A good example of 'Howard's Way' is provided by the events leading up to the Home Office Circular 18/1994 on the cautioning of offenders. During 1993, when the moral panic about juvenile crime was at one of its heights, stories and commentaries appeared in the broadsheets and tabloids critical of the extent to which cautioning had developed for young offenders. On the BBC *Public Eye* programme 'Cautionary Tales' (22 October 1993), a young offender talked of a caution meaning 'nothing', police officers spoke of rising crime as linked to rising cautions and of offenders laughing at the law; magistrates told of offenders not brought to justice . . . Actually, there was a case to be made that juvenile recorded crime had fallen, and multiple cautions were extremely rare, as were cautions for the more serious offences. Howard reacted by overriding the advice of his Home Office professional advisors, and reversed the policy developed since 1979. The outcome was Home Office Circular 18/1994, which established that offenders should normally only be cautioned once, except under special conditions. In spite of the evidence that cautioning did not lead to an increase in offending, Howard had decided 'your first chance should be your last chance' (Gibson 1995).

The pursuit of a policy of waging war on offenders in which justice equals revenge was to draw extensively on developments in the United States where punitiveness had developed apace. The custodial 'screw' was tightened in relation to youth offenders. The Criminal Justice and Public Order Act 1994 represents a significant step in reversing the non-custodial policies of the CJA 1991. The Act introduced secure training orders for juveniles aged 12 to 14 of up to two years, with five centres being planned to take

200 offenders. This was despite evidence to the effect that targeting persistent young offenders in this way would have negligible results (Hagell and Newburn 1994).

The CJPOA 1994 also gave powers to Crown Courts to order the long-term detention of 10- to 13-year-olds convicted of an offence which, had an adult committed it, could be punishable by a maximum of 14 years imprisonment (this provision had previously only applied to 14- to 17-year-olds). Further provisions included increasing the maximum sentences for detention of 15- to 17-year-olds, tightening of the law with regard to the granting of bail, the relaxation of requirements on the provision of PSRs prior to passing a custodial sentence. The detail here is important, for one must note the overall effect of the provisions was to make it easier for courts to lock up more young offenders for longer.

By 1994 Howard had visited Texas and returned with a proposal that US-style military 'boot camps' should be introduced in Britain to 'knock the criminal spirit out of young offenders' (*The Guardian* 2 June 1994). Reporting in *The Guardian* the same day on the initiative in the US, Martin Walker headlined with 'Effectiveness of strict regimes unproven but volunteer schemes catch public imagination'. Despite the manifest failure of the 'short sharp shock' experiment under William Whitelaw in the 1980s (Penal Affairs Consortium 1995), the thirst for 'revenge justice' (Rose 1995) remained unabated. By 1995 Mr Howard was attempting to persuade a reluctant MoD to accept young offenders into the Army Corrective Training Centre in Colchester (*The Times* 24 August 1995).

Nor did Mr Howard neglect punishment in the community: he sought to 'toughen' community sentences, ('Strengthening Punishment in the Community', Home Office 1995), revise National Standards for the Supervision of Offenders to tighten enforcement by supervising officers (Home Office 1995) and to increase the element of discipline in community sentencing by making the 'activities' more demanding and challenging. Howard argued that 'offenders should be punished not rewarded for their crimes' (*The Guardian* 10 March 1995). The requirement for probation officers to qualify via a Diploma in Social Work was abandoned in 1996. Mr Howard considered that former armed forces personnel had the 'relevant skills and experience to offer' and that they should not be disadvantaged by lack of a social work qualification. He called for 'punishment with a purpose' and argued that retired army officers 'understand the need for discipline and they won't stand any nonsense. That's exactly what young offenders need' (*The Guardian* 1 April 1995).

The last half of 1996 saw calls for a moral crusade around family values aimed at children and their parents. However, notably absent from the extensive discussion of moral and family values was any recognition that 'morality does not exist independently of social and economic relations' (Editorial, *Observer* 27 October 1997).

Then came Zero Tolerance: the ultimate policing solution. In an ironic turn of events, the original 'Zero Tolerance' campaign (a public awareness campaign aimed at heightening public sensitivity to the abuse of women and children) was forgotten in another favourite US import: zero tolerance policing. A form of proactive aggressive policing, this was introduced in selected parts of England based on the belief that if the police act on 'quality of life' offences, such as noise, rowdyism, criminal damage, drinking in public, swearing, dropping litter and so on, then the streets will be reclaimed for respectable citizens (Gibbons 1996; Johnston 1997). Young people, for obvious reasons (and see Chapter 5 in this volume) are often the target of such policies. In one version, employed in Hartlepool, the policy at the time of writing was to 'hit' youths – whether committing offences or not – on the streets, on the grounds that 'all crime begins on street corners' (Detective Chief Inspector Mallon, in *Daily Mail* 1 August 1996).

It is clear how the repressive policies and practices of the 1990s in particular construct young people as outsiders. As Vivien Stern pointed out, while other European countries tend to favour the reintegration of offenders into the community, Home Office press releases and government ministers 'use the language of conflict, contempt, and hatred'; 'doing good is a term of derision', and seeking to help offenders means that you 'do not care about the pain and suffering of victims' (Vivien Stern writing in *The Guardian* 2 May 1996).

Should one want a rational and utilitarian scale against which to measure the policy developments outlined here, it would be advisable to glance at the 1996 Audit Commission review of young people, crime and criminal justice (Audit Commission 1996). The Audit Commission has a government brief to make recommendations on the economy, effectiveness and efficiency of public sector agencies. The Commission found the youth justice system to be costly, inefficient and ineffective, and as failing both young people and their victims. The report draws attention to the need to develop preventative services for those at risk of offending. In dealing with youth crime the emphasis is on providing help and support for parents and families who find it difficult to cope. An array of unmet needs are identified in relation to housing, employment and training, leisure provision, and drug and alcohol problems. Cautioning was found to work well for first offenders and could be more widely used for second- and third-time offenders if more use was made of cautioning support schemes. It estimated that the number of young offenders prosecuted could be effectively reduced by 20 per cent. In respect of programmes for persistent young offenders the report noted the value of intensive behaviour-based and need-based programmes.

The government's response to the report was swift: the Home Office Minister, David McLean, dismissed the report as 'pathologically defeatist' and announced the government's intention to change the law to extend the electronic monitoring of offenders to juveniles.

New Labour, new punitiveness?

On 1 May 1997 the Conservative party was defeated in a Labour landslide general election victory. Is there any reason to expect a change in youth justice policy, as had happened under 'old Labour' governments? Even before the general election, as we have seen, New Labour was competing gamely for the law and order high ground. The then shadow Home Secretary, Jack Straw, jousted with Michael Howard in 'tough talk' about youth crime. The Labour party's support for many of Howard's contentious proposals facilitated the passage of the Crime (Sentences) Act 1997 through Parliament. In this last piece of legislation before the election, the courts were given powers to 'name and shame' juvenile offenders, and allowed the electronic monitoring of juveniles to enforce curfews.

Before and after the election, Mr Straw pursued the tactic of demonizing young people. Since becoming Home Secretary, he has indicated his priority is a 'root and branch' overhaul of the youth justice system. Drawing selectively on the 1996 Audit Commission report, he pointed to a 35 per cent increase in youth crime over the past decade and equated this with a 35 per cent fall in the numbers dealt with in court: unfortunately the implied connection (that crime increases when offenders are diverted rather than brought to court and punished) is invalid since the crime figures were drawn from the British Crime Survey whereas those relating to the courts were drawn from the Home Office Criminal Statistics. The new government's proposed Crime and Disorder Bill suggests parental responsibility orders; child protection orders to impose curfews on under-10s; community safety orders to 'restrain the antisocial behaviour of named individuals'; the abolition of *doli incapax*, thereby holding 10- to 13-year-olds fully responsible for their acts; a single 'warning' to replace the formal caution which will 'trigger' referral to multi-agency young offender teams; setting limits to the court's use of the discharge (i.e. to prevent them 'over'using it); 'reparation orders'; the development of more intensive community sentences; and the transfer of 17-year-olds from the youth court back to the adult court, thus reversing the provision of the 1991 Act (*The Guardian* 15 May 1997). Such proposals, if implemented, would widen considerably the net of social control by increasing the number of young people appearing in court; they would intensify intervention into the lives of young people and families not only for offenders but also in relation to children under 10, hitherto beyond the reach of the criminal law. More broadly, the inexorable focus of ministerial attention has been on the problem of juvenile behaviour, under-age drinking (including claims that youthful alcohol consumption is linked closely to a career in offending – in which case around a quarter of juveniles would become career offenders, whereas the actual proportion is probably more like 3 per cent – see Brown 1994a, for example), and the establishment of a Task Force on Youth Justice to 'overhaul' a system which Mr

Straw announced 'mimicked the behaviour of a bad parent – indulgent one minute, overly harsh the next' (*The Guardian* 22 May 1997).

Politics, policy talk and problem youth

Any explanation of the changes which have taken place in the youth justice system must give primacy to the influence of political beliefs and ideology. Hood (1974: 417) writes: 'the belief that expert advice based on criminological and penological research is the foundation for penal change, is only a screen behind which ideological and political factors, perhaps inevitably, shape those attitudes which imbue legislation'.

While the influence of criminology has been marginal on the ways in which society views and responds to youth crime, an appeal to penological theory and research has proved useful when it offers support to political objectives and ideological imperatives. This occurred during the 1960s when the Labour government sought to promote a welfare-based response to juvenile crime. Conversely criminological knowledge and research can be readily discounted or ignored when it appears to conflict with political objectives and ideological imperatives. This occurred when the Conservative government sought to promote a punishment-based response to juvenile crime in the 1980s. An emphasis on political beliefs and ideologies does not mean that legislative change is necessarily characterized by conflict. It is generally accepted that the development of a welfare-based juvenile justice system between 1908 and 1969 was largely consensual, in that the political parties, although differing about the speed of change and the means to achieve change, accepted the overall objective of the state provision of a comprehensive system of social welfare. Even during the 1970s, when cracks began to appear in the consensus, and the role of the state in the provision of social welfare began to be debated, the questioning did not lead to a fundamental reappraisal of the welfare-based Children and Young Persons Act 1969. The election of a Conservative government in 1979 inaugurated the beginning of a long period during which political ideology has become increasingly the dominant force in determining criminal justice and youth justice policies. While Windlesham (1993: 106) argues there are 'few restraints on a Home Secretary's freedom of action', he recognizes that governments have always been especially sensitive to the views of the judiciary, the magistracy and the police. In addition governments pay close attention to the 'tabloid and middle market press' (p. 19) as an indicator of public opinion. In the 1990s, as the public's fear of crime and the politicians' fear of being seen as 'soft on crime' increase, so has the influence of the tabloid press grown. At the time of writing there are few signs that the fixation with punishment has run its course. For nearly 20 years scant attention has been paid to the possibility that crime might have social causes and there are no signs that New Labour is about to become 'tough on the causes of crime'.

Through the twists and turns of youth justice policy, we see a recurring and ongoing preoccupation with the perceived threat to social stability posed by unregulated, undisciplined and disorderly youth outside adult control. Youthful misbehaviour has come to be regarded as symbolizing all that is wrong with adult society: family failure, inadequate parenting; all these perceptions have influenced policy proposals and legislative changes throughout the twentieth century.

Even though the '"normal" family has now narrowed to the structure of the nuclear unit' (Griffin 1993: 101), neither the diagnosis of the problem (the deficiencies of working class family life) nor the solutions (state intervention in various guises) have changed during the twentieth century. Both major political parties ignore the 'structural factors (housing, health, employment, education) that condition criminality' (Johnston 1997). Perhaps the 'political and cultural enterprise' (Hendrick 1990: 56) of the late twentieth century is the same as in the late nineteenth century. However, the modes of representation and response become ever more sophisticated and less tolerant:

> If we don't check yobbish behaviour, we create a licence to commit other crimes. Young people seem to feel they can do what they want and nobody's restraining them. We're saying there are limits to what society tolerates. If we deal with minor crime, it reinforces the idea of how to behave.
> (Barry Shaw, Cleveland Constabulary Chief Constable, in Gibbons
> 1996)

From the nineteenth century through to the present day, youth and youth justice policies have been rooted in the adult world, have reflected adult concerns with the threat of youth, and have been constructed to allay adult fears.

For many adults 'crime is seen as young people, and vice versa' (Brown 1995: 32). Perhaps it is understandable that 'crime' and 'young people' are bracketed together given the way media and politicians have fanned the flames of popular anxieties. However, whether the youth justice policies developed have been based on care or control, welfare or justice, treatment or punishment, they have reflected adult society's view of what is in the best interests of young people. The perception that young people are immature and are (or should be) dependent upon their 'carers' has underpinned legislation and policy-making. The consequences of such beliefs can be seen in the way in which society reacts to young people as victims (as we shall see in Chapter 5). Despite the virulent punishment culture surrounding youth crime, the question of adult crime against children and young people is barely raised.

Further reading

Most of the references provided within the text of this chapter would form appropriate further reading on the specific issues. On the 1960s, see Harris and Webb (1987), Morris and Giller (1987) and Parsloe (1978). The former two texts are rather more theoretical and analytical; the latter is a historical survey. Millham *et al.* (1978), Harwin (1982) and Pitts (1988) provide various insights into the 1970s. For the transition from the 1970s to the 1980s, see Morris *et al.* (1980), Thorpe *et al.* (1980) and Morris and Giller (1987); on the 1980s, King (1991). Windlesham (1993) and Rutherford (1996) are useful contextualized accounts of developments up to the 1990s.

chapter five

'Punishing youth': victims or villains?

**Throwing away the key: punishment, politics, press and the
  public**
**Young people as victims I: 'behind closed doors' and wilful
  ignorance**
Young people as victims II: the other side of the youth crime coin
**The murky waters of golden pasts: accounting for collective
  myopia**
Further reading

In Chapter 3 we charted the processes of successive media 'demonizations'
of young people under modernity, and suggested that these particular ways
of 'repackaging reality' reflected and reinforced a long history of excluding
and silencing the young which militates against 'youth' being seen as anything other than society's 'villain'.

In this chapter we take up these themes in the context of a dualism we
have termed 'victims and villains'. We aim to explore the ways authoritarianism operates at the level of politics, media commentary and popular
opinion. We shall suggest that this both reflects and perpetuates a conceptualization of youth and crime which masks alternative realities and
silences alternative voices. In particular we look at the relatively scant
attention paid to the victimization of children and young people, despite
recent studies which suggest that the young are, indeed, 'more sinned
against than sinning' (Hartless *et al.* 1995). The comparative lack of
research – and lack of interest – in young victims goes hand in hand with the
massive preoccupation with young people as offenders: all are seemingly
inextricable from a general culture of punishment towards young people,
that further compounds their invisibility as victims.

In attempting to understand some of the key ways in which this situation
is produced and maintained, we shall frame our discussion within the
problematics of citizenship for young people, and within the overlapping

institutions and ideologies of the state and the family as modes of government. Finally, we shall consider the implications of these analyses for our understanding of youth and crime.

Throwing away the key: punishment, politics, press and the public

John Redwood, speaking as the Conservative government's Welsh Secretary in 1993, called for a 'crusade for commonsense' in the fight against crime:

> Home truths that once seemed banal do need to be reasserted . . .
> People are keener than ever to return to some bedrock of commonsense
> and certainty . . . Reasserting traditional values is not some antiquarian nicety, nor some new political initiative here today and forgotten
> tomorrow. Traditions cannot be manufactured by press release. They
> are in the blood.
>
> (*The Guardian* 13 November 1993)

Redwood was providing support for Prime Minister John Major's call for a return to 'back to basics' decencies, in particular, he continued, that 'children should be instilled with the fear of punishment for wrong-doing'. His assertions were an intriguing blend of political expediency, wishful thinking, and accuracy – if 'accuracy' is taken as the extent to which his sentiments mirrored the values promulgated by the press and their relationship to the prevalent 'structures of feeling' (Pearson 1983, 1985) in 1990s Britain. For this may not be regarded simply as an attempt by the Conservative party to hold on to the 'law and order' high ground which helped gain them the 1979 election and a subsequent nearly 18 years in government. Throughout the 1990s the press and the public's voracious appetite for punishing the young has remained constant, making the decade one of the historically buoyant eras for punitiveness (Carlen 1996; Cavadino and Dignan 1997).

As we have shown in Chapter 4, this can be demonstrated by the successive stream of proposed initiatives and legislation to curb young criminals, most particularly since the abduction and murder of James Bulger (see Chapter 3). The Criminal Justice and Public Order Bill, published 17 December 1993, proffered a 'three pronged' increase in the severity of sentences for juvenile offenders (*Independent* 18 December 1993). The *Independent* commented,

> The measures . . . are seen by the Government as a response to widespread concerns over juvenile offending. Michael Howard, the Home Secretary, said 'Many communities suffer terribly from the activities

of a handful of young hooligans who offend time and time again. They
are a menace to their communities'.

(*Independent* 18 December 1993)

Ironically, the controversy surrounding the Bill, as Ben Adler pointed
out, tended to emphasize the regulation of popular music and the 'right to
rave', so that

> The proposals for young offenders have gone largely unnoticed,
> despite opposition from all groups concerned with young offenders . . .
> The Bill . . . introduces a new sentencing measure, the secure training
> order, to deal with persistent young offenders . . . Five of these pri-
> vately run centres (whose primary concern will be security and con-
> finement) will be created, with places for 200 young people between
> the ages of 12 and 14 years.

(*The Guardian* 26 August 1994)

Despite a setback to Mr Howard's crusade in 1996 when both Appeal
Court judges and the European Court of Human Rights found him to be
unlawful in increasing the Lord Chief Justice's recommended sentence for
Venables and Thompson from 10 to 15 years, the Home Secretary remained
unabashed in his pursuance of the scourge of child criminals: in 1997, with
an election pending, a Green Paper was unveiled proposing curfews for
under-10s. Proposed Parental Control Orders would empower magistrates
to order parents to control children under 10 who were deemed 'at risk' of
becoming persistent offenders. Conditions would include night curfews,
accompanying children to and from school, or even staying at home to
impose the curfew.

From 1 May 1997, the Labour Government has continued in the same
spirit, showing that punitiveness toward young people is a much broader
and deeper issue than one of party politics. As noted in Chapter 4, the new
government's proposals for a Crime and Disorder Bill include parental
responsibility orders, child protection orders to impose curfews, a reduction in juvenile cautioning, and a removal of the presumption that 10- to
13-year-olds would be incapable of telling right from wrong (*The Guardian*
15 May 1997).

It is not so much the specific proposals for juvenile and youth punishment
which concern us here, but the framing of 'punishment' as the predominant
mode of governmental and popular response to young people. De Haan
(1990: 112) points out that the concept of punishment was originally a
feudal one which meant being 'treated like a slave'. It is quite distinct from
the concept of sanctions. Punishment, argues de Haan (following Nils
Christie 1985), 'intends inflicting pain, suffering or loss and so excludes
other sanctions from consideration' (de Haan 1990: 112). The philosophies
and languages of penalty form a large and complex area which is beyond

the scope of this book (see, for example, Duff and Garland 1994; Hudson 1996). For present purposes we are concerned with two 'levels' of the punitive response to the young: firstly, the insistent emphasis on the need to control youth crime through punishment in the penal sense (Hudson 1996: Chapter 1) and, secondly, the notion of punishment as a broader cultural response to young people inside and outside the formal institutions of the state. The two facets of punitive culture, of course, reflect and reinforce each other.

It is quite clear that the framing of provisions for responding to youth crime, along with most public discourse on the subject, takes place within a language of punishment. The predominance of 'punishment' as a cultural response in Britain particularly, means that young people are mostly seen as criminals deserving of punishment, rather than as citizens entitled to justice. As Carlen argues, 'questions of the democratic state's right to punish are necessarily bound up with issues of citizenship . . . a moral reciprocity is set up: the state is to satisfy the minimum needs of citizens and protect their lives and property from attack; citizens are to obey the law and to carry out other civic responsibilities laid upon them by virtue of their citizenship' (1996: 2). The delineating feature of the punishment culture is that by sleight of hand it proclaims from the rooftops the need to punish young people, to inflict pain, as a legitimate response to their wrongdoings against the citizenship of others (i.e. adults), while simultaneously denying or suppressing the reality that young people themselves are barely accorded citizenship rights. Just as the 1990s has seen an escalation in punitiveness, it has seen a corresponding diminution in the already scanty citizenship 'rights' accorded to the young. This is neatly captured in Carlen's 'political criminology' of youth homelessness. The young homeless – penalized, stigmatized and criminalized – are responded to as a 'problem population' of outsiders, a particularly vilified sector of the already vilified youth population. The punitive social culture almost completely ignores the fact that many of their 'careers' into homelessness, and the resultant survivalism (Carlen 1996) which can bring them into conflict with the law, began with criminal victimization *of* them (such as sexual and physical assault within the familial home), and was compounded by the successive failure of the state to deliver minimum levels of protection or provision. Hence,

> During the 1980s the British state failed to meet the minimum standards of increasing numbers of young citizens at the same time targeting them for receipt of tighter disciplinary controls, and, in the 1990s, even harsher punishments. During the same period it was revealed that while young persons suffer criminal victimization on a large scale, the crimes committed against them are seldom redressed . . . Instead of a moral reciprocity of citizen rights, there is an asymmetry of citizenship,

with young people being punished for not fulfilling their citizenship obligations even though the state fails to fulfil its duties of nurturance and protection towards them.

(Carlen 1996: 2)

A further issue within this is the resistance within the punitive culture to the notion of 'rights' for children and young people. In 1989 the General Assembly of the United Nations adopted the UN Convention treaty on the Rights of the Child (UNRC). The UK government ratified the treaty in 1991, meaning that the government is committed to 'ensure that the minimum standards set out in the Convention are met' (Save the Children, no date given; see also Roche 1997). These include the right to freedom of thought (Article 14), the right to freedom of association (Article 15), the right for children to be listened to in matters which affect them – including court proceedings and other official proceedings (Article 12), and that in all actions concerning a child, the child's 'best interests' should be a primary consideration (Article 3) (United Nations 1989). In January 1995 (preceding several of the legislative measures discussed above), a UN monitoring committee produced an eight-page report listing numerous UK policies and social conditions which were incompatible with the 54 articles of the Convention. These included (in a list 39 paragraphs long) the continuing legal status accorded to the smacking of children, proposals for secure training orders for 12- to 14-year-olds, the retention of the age of criminal responsibility at the age of 10 (with the exception of Scotland, the lowest in Europe), and the extent of homelessness and poverty among Britain's children. It recommended an independent body be set up in the UK to monitor the implementation of the Convention, and the establishment of a children's Ombudsman. The report also recommended that children's rights should form part of the school curriculum, and part of the training of the police, judges, social workers, health care workers, and staff in care and detention institutions (*The Guardian* 28 January 1995).

The scepticism, and indeed outrage, with which these criticisms were received in the UK by the press and politicians demonstrates clearly enough the contemptuous dismissal with which attempts to broaden citizenship for the young are greeted. The valid criticisms of the UNRC made by some advocates of children's rights – i.e. that the 'rights' contained within it are not rights in the strict legal sense (Roche 1997: 52), therefore it may be seen as a somewhat cosmetic exercise; and that the articles of the UNRC display internal contradictions which render their implementation problematic (p. 52) – were largely drowned by the voices of the outraged 'smacking never did me any harm' contingent. Not to overstate the argument, it must be acknowledged that despite this rather dismal picture, some extension of children's rights was potentially achieved through the 1989 Children Act. These, however, were narrow gains which relate principally to specific issues of the management of child welfare cases (see Roche 1997: 50–1 for a summary). Overall, the punitive culture surges on unabated.

It is the broader cultural resonance of punitiveness in the UK which encourages and enables politicians to define 'youth' as a problem to adult society rather than as citizens, so that children and young people are legislatively placed outside 'society' proper insofar as any notion of social contract or citizenship is involved. Through an unholy alliance, the popular media generally operate in tandem with this 'moral' climate. 'Boot camps' may never have been practicable, but as symbolic and rhetorical devices for channelling adult fears, they gained great popular currency, and it seems likely that equivalent languages and preoccupations will live on. The following sections explore some of the more complex and detailed elements in the maintenance of punitive desire. This necessitates locating the victimization of children and young people within, on the one hand, the domains of the family and the welfare state; on the other, within the domains of public space and policing.

Young people as victims I: 'behind closed doors' and wilful ignorance

> Historically children appeared as victims for only a very short period of time alongside the appearance of childhood as a separate and protected stage in the life cycle. During the twentieth century this way of viewing children largely became entangled in viewing them as offenders . . .
>
> (Walklate 1989: 58)

In this section we consider some of the victimization experiences of children and young people which form a familiar part of our media diet, emphasizing how they are framed in such a way as to prevent them being seen as part of the legitimate concerns of criminology or victimology, thus preventing them from affecting the dominant conception of youth as offenders.

Child victimization within the family

Firstly, there are the areas of victimization commonly characterized as child 'abuse' (physical or sexual) within familial settings (Walklate 1989: Chapter 3). For many young people, the family is a 'place of danger' (Muncie and McLaughlin 1996).

Despite a wealth of academic research in this area and recurrent media attention, such research, and such attention, has typically avoided conceptualizing child abuse as crime: indeed, 'a good deal of the research which has been conducted on child abuse has been concerned with issues of practice

. . . and the management of abuse cases' (Walklate 1989: 58). Child victimization in familial settings are fenced off as 'special' cases which are treated more as the concern of social work, medicine or psychiatry than the criminal justice system or criminology. This has occurred in a number of ways.

Child sexual abuse within the family in particular is treated within a vocabulary of 'dubiousness' or 'difficulty'. It is assumed that children are unreliable witnesses; the burden of proof may be placed on 'conflicting' scientific evidence; or, where the evidence is gathered from adults, 'false memory syndrome' may be invoked: for the criminal justice system 'deals with evidence and views retraction as evidence of telling lies. This obviously works against the interests of the child if the system fails to recognize the processes involved in normal adaptation to abuse. The image of the malevolent child appears again' (Walklate 1989: 75). This in turn relates to a broader social conception of children as liars or untrustworthy raconteurs (we shall return to this issue below).

The Cleveland Child Abuse cases of 1987 raised further central issues regarding judicial and societal evasion of child victimization. After the introduction in Cleveland of a medical diagnostic technique known as 'reflex anal relaxation and dilation', confirmed cases of child sexual abuse rose from two in the year for 1986, to 104 between March and July 1987, with 90 referrals occurring in May and June (Walklate 1989: 65). Of 121 children examined by the two doctors carrying out the diagnoses, 70 per cent were removed from the home by place of safety orders.

Within months, public attention was being focused by the media on the abrogation of the rights of parents, on supposed 'conspiracy' campaigns between the two doctors, on the incompetencies of social workers (Campbell 1988). Stuart Bell, a local MP, fashioned himself as a one-man campaigner for the rights of parents, and particularly the rights of fathers, and launched a high level and highly personalized campaign against the doctors and social workers involved in the diagnoses and removal of children.

The continuing saga of the Cleveland child abuse case (dubbed the 'backlash backlash' in a recent three-part television programme, *The Death of Childhood*, Channel 4, May 1997) reveals that much original evidence against parents used in the Butler Sloss Inquiry into the affair was then not allowed to be submitted in the criminal prosecutions, so that in many cases children were returned to the homes of known abusers. Gerrard (*Observer Review* 25 May 1997) notes that, 'Ten years ago, 121 children in Cleveland were taken from their parents. The doctor who suspected sexual abuse was vilified and 96 were sent home. But to what? Second opinions have since confirmed 75 per cent of her diagnoses.'

This is testimony to the willingness on the part of politicians, the media and the public to embrace thankfully any suggestion that the scale of abuse is exaggerated. We are apparently unable to face the factual evidence to suggest that 'the happy family is a consoling myth . . . no matter what we discover about marital breakdown, infidelity, domestic violence and sexual abuse, still we cling to it' (Gerrard, in *Observer Review* 25 May 1997).

This evident climate of denial and invisibility make it extremely difficult to estimate the extent of child abuse. In a report for the NSPCC using only official registrations, Creighton and Noyes (1989, cited in Muncie and McLaughlin 1996: 194) found that over the period 1983 to 1987 the 'sexual abuse rate increased from 0.08 to 0.65 per thousand children'. In 1989, 23,000 new cases of child sexual abuse were registered; in 1993, 26,000 (p. 194). However sympathetic one is to labelling perspectives, the curious fact in the face of the available evidence is why there has been so *little* 'moral panic'.

Firstly and most obviously, abuses within the family are largely hidden victimizations. Moreover, the power to resist intervention into the 'privacy' of family life still remains a paramount social value in Britain, as was amply demonstrated throughout the Cleveland cases. The 'policing of families' (Donzelot 1980), although extending the network of the social surveillance and regulation of the poor, has not primarily concerned itself with the victimization of young people, but has rather been a history of strategies of the state to effect 'government through the family' (Donzelot 1980: this is discussed in more detail in Chapter 4 of this volume). Although the late nineteenth century saw some recognition of the concept of 'cruelty' to children, the difficulties which this was seen to pose to the preservation of the 'sanctity' of family life were never to be surmounted:

> A wall of denial . . . faces those who seemingly exposed the possible extent of this abuse; in other words when the dominant ideology of the patriarchal family structure is challenged. Within this ideology, children do not have rights. The accused parents were seen to have rights insofar as they were championed in their claims of innocence. Their potential as voters, at least was recognized . . .
>
> (Walklate 1989: 68, citing Campbell 1988)

The history of attempts to legislate against child victimization within the family has never approached the constant stream of law and order legislation for youth crime (see an excellent summary of these issues in Muncie and McLaughlin 1996: Chapter 5). As writers in this field have often noted, the national concern over cruelty to animals has been stronger than that over children (Walklate 1989). The more recent debate over family violence has tended to be allied with feminist-informed campaigns against violence towards women in private settings (Kelly and Radford 1987), and it must be acknowledged that since the 1960s, public campaigns (the most recent of which has been the 'Zero Tolerance' campaign, not to be confused with the public policing initiative) have been punctuated by strengthened legislation in the field of 'child protection'.

However, the 1969 Children and Young Persons Act, in its focus on the 'problem family', conflated the deprived and the depraved, treating 'children in need' and offending behaviour as virtually synonymous, the latter being a symptom of the former (Walklate 1989, and Chapter 4 in this volume). The 1989 Children Act, although approaching child welfare from a more rights oriented perspective (as noted above), was vociferously challenged as a 'Trojan Horse whereby the integrity and sanctity of family life are undermined' (Roche 1997: 53), and received with fears that 'the law has gone so far in advancing rights for children that family life itself is under threat' (p. 53).

Thus ambivalence towards 'child protection' remains the predominant feature of the debate over child abuse. Across the political spectrum, the extension of social work intervention has been questioned – either from a left perspective which opposes the further regulation of the lives of the poor and a permeation of social control further into the social body, or from a right perspective which stresses the rights of the parent and the right of privacy. The framing of 'child abuse' as a 'family matter', with an emphasis on the welfare rather than the criminal justice system, as Morgan and Zedner note, 'may well obscure the fact that a criminal offence has been committed. The tendency to marginalize children as victims of crime is reinforced by the use of the term "abuse" rather than "assault"' (Morgan and Zedner 1992: 20).

Thus any attempt to understand the 'fencing off' of child victimization in the family goes to the heart of the relationship between the family and the state, and the predominant cultural framing of the place of the child within the family. These complex issues are summarized nicely by Walklate (1989: Chapter 3) and Muncie and McLaughlin (1996: Chapter 5).

Victimization in care

The growth of social work intervention has also brought with it an escalating problem of victimization in care institutions. The assumption that a child is being removed from a dangerous family setting to a 'place of safety' has its own difficulties. Care institutions, in their role as 'substitute' family settings, are largely invisible bureaucratic sites for the control of troubled and troublesome children and young people. They are, by definition, controlling institutions operating on the basis of 'professional judgement' within legal parameters; the potential for abuses of power is therefore incipient within them.

It has been estimated that there are approximately 8000 children and young people living in residential settings administered by social services and education departments (Corby 1997: 210). As with familial settings, the common term for victimization in residential care is 'abuse' or alternatively 'mistreatment' (p. 211). Again, the framing of, and responses to, serious criminal victimization of children and young people has tended to be denied, subsumed under the discourse of the independent 'inquiry', or in some cases, deliberately concealed from public view. Despite spates of criminal prosecutions, the victimization of children and young people in care has not been responded to in the state or public domains as a 'crime problem'; rather, the problem has been conceptualized as either a 'bad apple' syndrome where 'bad or wicked individuals in authority are seen to take advantage of relatively powerless young people' (Corby 1997: 211), or as the unfortunate result of situations in which 'a policy goal approved by an institution is later judged to be abusive' (p. 211). These characterizations of victimization in care are revealed as highly inadequate, and indeed the readiness with which they are accepted (despite the identification of institutional abuse as a significant problem involving substantial numbers of children; see Westcott, cited in Corby 1997: 211) by the media and the public is once more indicative of much deeper problems in framing the youth crime problem. This may be seen in relation to a number of recent cases.

During the 1990s, media depictions of child abuse cases focused on projecting the 'evil' onto perversion rather than ordinariness (e.g. *The Guardian* 27 May 1992, 14 July 1992, 15 July 1992, 6 April 1996, *Observer* 21 April 1996). 'Paedophilia', rather than victimization arising out of the everyday relationships between children and adults or the nature of institutional cultures, becomes the favoured discourse. Even here, much of the coverage warns against taking the issue 'too far', as in Barry Hugill's *Observer* coverage of a court case that 'cleared eight defendants but closed a children's home run by Quakers': 'ABUSE CASE PUT HUGGING ON TRIAL' ran the headline (21 April 1996). One might be forgiven for thinking that no occurrence of child abuse in the home had taken place. Yet the piece further reveals that children in the home had been kept in solitary confinement; that in April 1992 police officers had intercepted child pornography posted to a childcare expert and consultant to the school, Peter Righton, who was living with the principal of the school, Richard Alston; that Alan Stewart, a member of staff, was charged in April 1993 with sexually assaulting three girls under 14 and subsequently jailed for four years. But, claims Hugill:

> At issue was the right of residential care workers to hug and hold children. It posed questions of discipline, affection, and punishment, illustrating the fear of paedophilia that haunts police and social workers . . . the school was run on democratic principles . . . It housed children rejected by other homes, many so disturbed that they were a danger to themselves and others . . .

Hugill details the 'good work' done by the school and implies that its closure was part of a dangerous tendency to make a moral panic out of the occasional 'bad apple'.

Even a casual reading of the reports of recent episodes suggests a far more complex picture. The 1990s have seen a wave of child abuse scandals in care homes suggesting a scale and an invisibility of abuse which implies both widespread institutional complicity and even organized 'paedophile rings'. Discussing the case of the official inquiry into care homes in Cheshire, Roger Dobson writes:

> Detectives have explored the idea that the perpetrators of these crimes belonged to organized paedophile networks, but they have been hampered by the refusal of all the convicted abusers to talk . . . 'There have to be some links (said one Officer) – everyone networks at some stage – but no one has ever said anything'.
>
> (*Independent on Sunday* 9 June 1996)

Similarly in Clwyd, a series of 14 separate inquiries were held but the results were withheld from the public. Despite public horror over cases of random and savage attacks on children by 'monsters', the reaction to abuse in institutions has been much more cautious. As Dobson notes,

> Cheshire may be the biggest scandal so far, but there are grounds for believing that we might have woken up to the dangers in our children's homes long ago . . . the abuse in Staffordshire occurred in the 1980s and compensation claims were made in 1992 . . . The scandal of Frank Beck, who abused dozens of children in care in Leicestershire between 1973 and 1986, became known to the public when he was prosecuted in 1991 . . . The Clwyd abuse scandal emerged in the early 1990s and subsequently led to a police investigation lasting two years in which 300 cases were referred to the Crown Prosecution Service . . .
>
> (*Independent on Sunday* 9 June 1996)

Earlier in the year, the *Independent* had also reported on another interesting aspect of the Clwyd case: a leading insurance company had tried to prevent the Jillings Inquiry (the independent inquiry commissioned into the affair) taking place, claiming that it would be a 'hostage to fortune' and a 'dress rehearsal to claimants' (*Independent* 6 April 1996). Councillors appointed the independent inquiry team 'in response to fears that a paedophile ring had taken hold in children's home over a twenty year period of abuse', but we are told that the insurer's response was to threaten the council with an invalidation of cover. They also allegedly prevented councillors from seeing a full report of an earlier investigation, sought to control claims to the Criminal Injuries Compensation Board, and 'blocked the routine practice of placing public notices in newspapers seeking information from former residents and staff'. The company, it seems, feared legal claims from victims. Meanwhile, 'the Welsh Social Services Inspectorate did not inspect a single home. The Inspectorate is quoted as saying in 1992 that "There is no evidence to suggest that this problem [child sex abuse] occurs frequently"' (*Independent* 6 April 1996).

At issue, again, is the assumption that young people in care are essentially *offenders*. Little distinction is made between categories of residential incarceration, so that in the public imagination at least, there is little to choose between a secure unit housing young offenders and a care home housing young people who may well have ended up there because they were initially victims of criminal offences.

The question of the rights of children in homes is viewed dimly; control regimes bordering on or including criminal victimization are legitimated because of the supposed 'nastiness' of the 'inmates', and clear cases of institutional complicity and hints of organized crime are passed over. Following the conclusions of a Gulbenkian Foundation working group of 1993, Corby comments:

> There is need for more emphasis on the positive principles of caring for children and young people rather than on the means of controlling them. In the current climate where the government is setting up secure training centres for persistent young offenders between the ages of 12 and 14, the outlook on this front is bleak.
>
> (Corby 1997: 212)

Young people as victims II: the other side of the youth crime coin

As we have previously argued, children and young people in western modernity have generally been accorded legitimate 'victim' status within very narrow parameters. This has been either at the extremes of 'private' violence – child cruelty and latterly, child sexual abuse in the family – or as 'innocent' victims of psychotic stranger violence (as with abductions, or attacks in schools such as Dunblane). In this section we wish to examine what, if possible, is an even more controversial issue: the notion of children as 'normal' victims of 'normal' crimes. Until the 1990s, a growing interest in victim studies in the UK had largely ignored children (but see Mawby 1979 for an exception). As Goodey comments:

> Children under sixteen years of age are often disqualified from participation in much of social science research . . . Too often children's role within criminological studies is seen as 'offender' while in the eyes of the media the child is regarded as victim, for example, of a sex attack or incest.
>
> (Goodey 1994: 195)

Victimization surveys are particularly significant here because, unlike the police crime statistics, they go some way to uncovering the 'dark figure' of unreported or unrecorded crime (Coleman and Moynihan 1996). Although adopting differing methodologies, such surveys typically take a representative sample from a general population and use structured interviews to gather information on individuals' experiences of a wide range of victimization over a given period of time. Despite several valid criticisms of the technique (Zedner 1994; Coleman and Moynihan 1996), victim surveys have provided extremely interesting insights into the nature and extent of everyday victimization, particularly among the most powerless or fearful sections of the population, who are unlikely to report. National victim surveys were adopted by the Home Office with the first sweep of the British Crime Survey in 1981 and subsequently in 1982, 1984, 1988, 1992, 1994 and 1996. Only in 1994 did the Home Office begin to include younger people aged 12–15, largely due to the innovative work carried out in the late 1980s by a research team based at Edinburgh University (Anderson *et al.* 1994; Home Office 1995). Up until this point, child victimization in the general rather than the 'special' or 'sexualized' sense had not been considered an issue in the British context (Morgan and Zedner 1992). Intrigued by the emergent findings of the Edinburgh survey (discussed further below), researchers in Glasgow in 1990 (Hartless *et al.* 1995) and in Teesside in 1992 (Brown 1994a, 1995) undertook verificational studies with 11- to 15-year-olds. All three surveys produced startlingly similar results. With sample sizes of 1150 (Edinburgh), 208 (Glasgow, research carried out in the same sample areas in Edinburgh as Anderson *et al.*) and 1000 (Teesside), in different regions – indeed, different countries – carried out and analysed independently using varied questionnaires and by different research teams, the consistency of the results underscores a number of key issues in youth victimization generally.

All three surveys found high levels of harassment of young people by adults, defined as staring, following on foot, following by car, 'asking' things, shouting, or threatening; and even higher levels of victimization of young people by other young people. Significant levels of victimization for more serious offences, including physical assault and theft from the person, were also revealed in all the studies. In Brown's study for example, nearly half the sample had been the victim of harassment from other young people in the year preceding the survey; nearly one quarter had been physically attacked by another young person, and one in twelve had been a victim of theft from the person (Brown 1995a: 36). As regards victimization of young people by adults, over half had experienced harassment, 7 per cent had been physically attacked, and 5 per cent had experienced theft from the person (p. 37). Again, these figures are commensurate with the Scottish surveys, and become even more startling when reanalysed by age category and gender. In all three studies, the relatively low levels of reporting to the police (compared with adult surveys) and the relatively high levels of fear engendered by victimization, suggest that the experience was far from trivial in many instances. Brown, who also conducted a victimization study with adults over the same period, found considerably lower levels of victimization of adults, and concluded that young people endured levels of victimization which would not be tolerated by adults. Similarly, Hartless *et al.* (1995) categorically refuted the notion that victimization of young people was 'child's play'.

The British Crime Survey findings produced lower, but still substantial, levels of victimization of 12- to 15-year-olds, using an instrument based to some extent on Anderson *et al.* (Home Office 1995). This is probably due in part to methodological differences: for example, the Edinburgh and Teesside studies were carried out in schools but without teachers present, thus enhancing confidentiality, whereas the BCS was carried out at the family home; the Edinburgh and Teesside questions on some items were phrased more loosely, and the BCS included victimization at school and home, whereas the Edinburgh and Teesside studies focused only on public places (see Home Office 1995). Nevertheless, despite such disparities, the BCS study conceded that the patterns of victimization in the BCS and the Edinburgh study were similar (Home Office 1995).

These findings show conclusively that, despite young peoples' undoubted widespread involvement in petty offending (a fact which none of the cited studies attempts to dispute), their role in serious offending is minor (Anderson *et al.* 1994; Brown 1994a) and is far outweighed by their vulnerability as victims. Yet adults, whether as politicians, journalists and programme-makers, or as the general public, are far more concerned with the 'lack' of secure units, the 'terrorizing' of estates by young 'thugs' and the lack of 'discipline' in modern society. This is also despite consistent findings from numerous surveys which demonstrate that young peoples' attitudes on a number of measures of social attachment, such as law and order, education, the environment and the family, show them to be, if anything, *more* socially concerned than adults (e.g. Furnham and Gunter 1989; Brown 1994a; Guardian/ICM 1996). We are not concerned here to engage with the debate which may be summarized as 'but what do we do about the hard core of persistent young offenders who wreak havoc'; for this is in itself part of the sleight of hand which repeatedly shows an adult population in denial. The question should rather be one of *why*, despite a mass of carefully gathered empirical evidence suggesting the need for a whole range of policies which support community safety for young people, the prominent discourse is, quite literally, 'victim blaming' (Griffin 1993).

The murky waters of golden pasts: accounting for collective myopia

The accounts of victimization discussed above, then, sit very uneasily with the tenacious adherence to a punishment culture which appears to be central to contemporary British societal attitudes. The overwhelming evidence is that society barely recognizes young people's vulnerability to crime, refuses to acknowledge the status of adults as overwhelmingly the perpetrators of crime, and refuses to loosen its attachment to the framing of 'youth' as the villain. There are a number of ways in which it may be possible to account for the persistence of the punishment culture and the denial of youth victimization, all of which have some degree of plausibility.

The first possibility is that punitiveness towards the young is an essentially understandable, if not exactly rational, response by the adult world to the actual problem of youth crime. Such a position would be compatible with 'radical realism' in criminology (Matthews and Young 1992; Young and Matthews 1992; Young 1994). Young has claimed that a crisis has arisen in criminology partly from a refusal by criminologists to take crime seriously: that is, by playing down the importance of discovering the causes of crime, and by failing to recognize the real effects of crime on everyday life. Later on in this section, we shall be deploying this argument in relation to young people as victims of crime; here, however, we wish to examine the implications of radical realism for understanding adult punitiveness towards young people. Despite all that has been said in this book about the 'scapegoating' of young people, it remains true that young people are also commonly offenders. As we have pointed out, none of the studies of young people and crime which have stressed the victimization of young people has attempted to wave away the picture suggested by the official statistics, that there is a powerful association between youth and offending behaviour (Braithwaite 1989). Indeed, the studies cited in the earlier part of this chapter, particularly that of Anderson *et al.* (1994), may themselves be loosely located within the realist perspective, in that they also studied young people as offenders and witnesses of crime. Thus, just as Home Office criminal statistics repeatedly show peak ages of known offenders to be between 15 and 18 years of age (Coleman and Moynihan 1996), the self-report questions in Anderson *et al.* (1994) and Brown (1994a) show that petty offending among 11- to 15-year-olds is so common as to be almost 'normal'. Anderson *et al.* comment that official statistics of youthful offending cannot be taken seriously – because they 'are a ridiculous *understatement*' (1994: 88).

Can the admittedly wide extent of petty offending among teenagers be used to help explain the persistence of the punishment culture? One application of the realist argument would suggest that the answer to this is 'yes'. To understand this, we must return to the studies of adult victims carried out by radical realists before youth victimology was raised. The initial implementation of the British Crime Survey provoked a realist critique in taking a national sample, the BCS had the impact of disguising not only specific localized pockets of victimization within certain areas but also particular subsections of the (adult) population. Hence local victim studies of adult populations in areas such as Islington, Merseyside, Teesside and Edinburgh (Kinsey 1985; Jones *et al.* 1986; Brown 1992; Anderson *et al.* 1994) showed that in deprived inner city areas, the effects of crime, even 'petty' crime, could have highly deleterious effects on vulnerable sections of the population. Victimization was found to be disproportionately distributed in already deprived areas, so that contrary to a once-common wisdom, it was the economically disadvantaged resident in public housing (for example), or the socially discriminated-against groups, such as ethnic minorities and women, who were more likely to be victims of crime than the socially and economically powerful. Moreover, the effects of victimization were also disproportionately felt by those who were vulnerable, whether economically, physically or psychologically (poor people, women, ethnic minorities, elderly people, people with disabilities). The reasons for this are fairly obvious: a lack of economic resources and social power rendered such groups less able to protect themselves against victimization (e.g. the protection to property afforded by expensive security systems, the personal protection afforded by being able to travel in private rather than public transport, or by physical strength). The same disadvantages also increased the effects of crime (e.g. the economic impact of property crime on people already in poverty, the psychological impact on the frail or elderly). The Merseyside study in particular (Kinsey 1985) also highlighted the importance of differential access to effective policing. Put simply, among populations where the quality of life was already low, crime was highest and had the greatest effect.

If we apply these findings to the phenomenon of young people as offenders, most of whose offences consisted of incivilities, criminal damage, theft and offences concerning motor vehicles (Anderson *et al.* 1994; Brown 1994a), then it becomes easier to see why the apparently 'minor' crimes of the young become anything but minor in their effects on adults. It is true that it is very often the young who perpetrate precisely those quality of life offences which form the proverbial last straw for people who already have nothing. Qualitative research captures the flavour of this problem in a way which shows how patronizing the categorization of offences as 'petty' can be. For example, in one study,

> The first time I planted vegetables, and they took those. Then I put some flowers and shrubs in – they waited until they just got established and they took those. I've grown this Christmas tree and I'm taking it in before it's ready or they'll take that. The garden is the only thing I've

got, it's my only outlet, but I'll just give up now and grow a few plants indoors.

(Single parent, victim of local young people, in Brown 1992: 42)

Or again, 'They wrecked the furniture but [child] needs it . . . he suffers from Cerebral Palsy . . . they wrote "spacca" all over the walls . . . that's what hurts the most' (single parent, victim of local young people, in Brown 1992: 37).

Numerous repeated incidents of damage to gardens, fences and cars, and even incivilities such as calling 'coffin dodgers' after elderly people (p. 37) or being sworn at by children, are draining and depressing to people who are already finding living a struggle. Moreover, young people are highly *visible*: much of their offending behaviour occurs in groups and in public, a fact which in itself increases adult anxiety. As Young (1992: 49–50) comments, 'what can be more central to the quality of life than the ability to walk down the street at night without fear, to feel safe in one's own home, to be free from harassment and incivilities in the day-to-day experience of urban life?'

For a number of reasons, however, these arguments are insufficient. Firstly, they do not sufficiently recognize the damage done by the crimes which are entirely or predominantly those of adults: environmental crimes, serious burglaries, rape, murder, pension fraud, and so on. In constructing the 'effects' literature in the way it does, realism is far from 'true to the nature of crime' (Young 1992). The effect and visibility of youthful offending in itself is not enough to explain the persistence of the punishment culture. We must also consider the parallel question of why the victimization of young people is so effectively downplayed, resulting in a failure to challenge the punitive frame and retaining this obsession with youth crime.

Here, indeed, realism can be turned around upon itself. It is no accident that youth victimization studies arose in part from radical realists themselves (Anderson *et al.* 1994). Most of the points made above in relation to victimization of adults could equally – if not with more justification – be applied to the young. Yet youth victimization is rarely taken seriously (Morgan and Zedner 1992). Young people, as we have demonstrated, are a disadvantaged group; their fear of crime is commensurate with their actual experiences as victims of it; they are relatively powerless (including economic marginality, lack of citizenship status or 'personhood', non-enfranchisement). This is in *addition* to the disadvantages of power – divisions of gender, ethnicity, disability and poverty – experienced by adults. Young peoples' vulnerability is actually *exacerbated* by the ways in which childhood and youth have been constructed. They are not only highly likely to become victims of crime, but their relationship to the adult world renders them less able to protect themselves against crime, renders them more susceptible to its effects, and renders them less likely to be accorded a legitimate voice and therefore to receive adequate support or protection. In relation to policing in particular, their complicated social positioning as offenders, witnesses *and* victims makes their access to effective adult protection problematic. This has been represented by Anderson *et al.* (1994: 158) as a 'vicious circle of young people and crime' whereby adults are indifferent to the victimization of young people and police do not take it seriously, young people develop their own strategies for coping with crime, some of which may involve them in offending, such as carrying weapons for protection, and others of which reinforce their invisibility, such as 'not grassing' – and the whole cycle of indifference/invisibility both reinforces their vulnerability and makes it more likely that they will primarily be characterized as offenders (p. 158). Their characterization as primarily offenders then feeds the notion that we must take (youth) crime seriously, to a further preoccupation with the aetiology of youthful offending, to a further criminological and policy preoccupation with 'youth as problem' and 'youth as other' . . . and so the cycle is reinforced. Thus although the punitive culture is partly explicable in terms of the *real* effects of youth crime, mediated through inequalities of power experienced by its victims, we must also acknowledge the complex processes whereby youth crime is constructed as the 'predominant' problem precisely through the processes of rendering invisible the victimization of the young; this then becomes a crucial factor in the maintenance of punitiveness.

We have noted above some of the ways in which this process happens in the context of the everyday, public acts of victimization. However, as we have touched upon in the preceding section, public acts of victimization are only one side of the story. The welfare and the criminal justice systems both operate to reinforce particular conceptions of the 'victim' and the 'villain', so that child victims are not considered in a comparable way to adult victims. For all the increased concentration of victims of crime in recent years,

> The victimization of children is seen solely in terms of child abuse . . . In the criminal justice system allegations of child abuse are treated in a different way from other types of allegation . . . as a result, interest and concern about child victimization has developed largely outside a criminological framework.
>
> (Morgan and Zedner 1992: 6)

Children and young people have to *earn* their status as victims (p. 6), whereas they are eagerly *ascribed* their status as offenders. This dualism operates at several levels; the popular (see Chapter 3), the political, the policy level (Chapter 4), and the academic (Chapter 2).

More broadly, the punitive culture towards young people must be seen as rooted in a long history in which the 'chastisement' of children is the legitimate province of the family as a primary institution of socialization and control. 'Discipline' by parents (or rather the lack of it) has so consistently been placed at the forefront of debates about the crime problem that we must consider whether there is a longstanding and deeply ingrained punitiveness towards children and young people which precedes, and frames, our societal insistence upon seeing young people as a problem population who must first and foremost be contained through punishment.

Further reading

On child victimization in familial settings see Campbell (1988), Walklate (1989) and Muncie and McLaughlin (1996: Chapter 5). On the victimization of young people in public space, see Anderson *et al.* (1994), Brown (1995) and Home Office (1995). Morgan and Zedner (1992) provide an interesting critique of the academic treatment of child victimization.

chapter six

Youth and crime: beyond the boy zone

Girls and crime: speaking into the silence
Boy-ness and crime: masculinities
Beyond the boy zone?
Further reading

At the heart of the youth crime nexus is the boy zone. In criminological research and theory 'youth and crime' has been largely defined by an over-riding concern with the young male offender. This has both reflected and fuelled popular and policy debates, notwithstanding the emergence of more recent critiques.

Returning for a moment to Chapter 2, it cannot have gone unnoticed that all of the formative studies discussed focused virtually exclusively on boys as 'offenders' or 'delinquents'. Constituting the hub of youth criminology in Britain, both in terms of the production of theory and the choice of the discipline's subject-matter, all subsequent studies have then either unques-tioningly accepted, or had to take critical issue with, this body of 'standard' knowledge. Latour (1986) would characterize this as an 'obligatory pas-sage point': one is virtually forced to go through it in order to get anywhere else. In this way, *one* crime problem has become *the* crime problem insofar as young people are concerned (Coleman and Moynihan 1996: 111): that of male youthful offending.

Whether in the person of the bespectacled and besuited pre-war 'man of science' academic, or the 1970s eager young leather-jacketed radical aca-demic, or the 1980s football-fan-gone-native academic, most criminology has been written by men, about boys and young men. This tendency is not particularly difficult to understand. An explanation may be found within the wider context of the construction of adolescence and the 'marginal male' (see Chapter 1); in the composition of the criminological fraternity (*sic*) in the formative decades (Chapter 2); in the spectacle-value of young male crime (Chapter 3), and in the obsessions of youth crime policy, which although making provisions for both sexes, have always been ordered around the assumption that the 'normal offender' is the boy or young man (Chapter 4). The interlinking of these histories produced a situation where young males were assured a place as the focus of much criminology (for more detailed accounts of 'malestream' criminology see, for example, Smart 1976; Morris 1987).

Here we must deal with the common sense and the obvious: as we discussed in Chapter 5, it *is* the typical crimes of boys which have most impact on everyday perceptions of victimization and fear – or rather anxiety – about crime. In a consideration of a wide range of official data sources and criminological surveys, Coleman and Moynihan (1996: Chapter 5) conclude that 'we can state, with varying degrees of confidence, that known offenders are disproportionately likely to be young, male and lower class' (p. 110). From the 'realist' perspective (Young 1992), it is both logical and important to concentrate criminological attention in this way. However, there are a number of problems with this enterprise, some of which have begun to be addressed, and some of which have not.

In this chapter we shall examine the contributions which studies of girls/women and crime, and masculinities and crime, have made in taking us beyond the 'boy zone'; we conclude by looking at some of the absences which still exist in youth criminology.

Girls and crime: speaking into the silence

The virtual absence of girls and women in the history of criminology is now well documented (Smart 1976; Leonard 1982; Morris 1987; Heidensohn 1994). It is not that girls and women were entirely ignored, but that female criminality was '*relatively* neglected and was treated in certain very specific ways' (Heidensohn 1994: 999).

Thus early commentators on the gender dimension in criminogenesis tended to focus on the 'peculiar' characteristics of women which rendered them less crime prone or their criminal acts less discoverable – a tired history of biologism and sexism. (Box 1983: Chapter 5; Messerschmidt 1993: Chapter 1; and Heidensohn 1994 give readable accounts of the work of early criminologists on female crime.) In general, the assumptions running throughout these diverse works were either that if women did commit crime, then by definition their lack of femininity must be explained since it was not within the true nature of femininity to do so (Lombroso and Ferrero 1895); or, that femininity was productive of specific kinds of crime involving in particular a facility for deceitfulness which rendered these crimes relatively invisible (Pollak 1950). As criminology developed in empirical scope and theoretical sophistication, the study of female criminality was bypassed:

> The consequence of this was a scenario reminiscent of *Sleeping Beauty*. Whereas the rest of the criminological world moved on from positivism, embracing in particular a series of sociological theories of crime and deviance, female crime was cut off from most of this development as though by thickets of thorn . . .
>
> (Heidensohn 1994: 1000)

It was not until the late 1960s that questions began to be raised in any serious sense about female criminality (Heidensohn 1968), nor until the publication of Smart's *Women, Crime and Criminology* in the 1970s (Smart 1976) was an attempt made at a comprehensive treatment of women and crime. The subsequent decades have seen a massive expansion in research and theoretical work in the field. While the diversity of these contributions cannot be covered adequately here, there have been certain key ways of framing questions about 'women and crime' which it is important to explore.

One orientation has been to problematize control and conformity (Heidensohn 1996). Here, the question posed is based on the importance of understanding the relative conformity of women compared with men. Developing from the work of Hirschi (1969), control theory reverses the question of why people deviate by posing the question of why people conform. In this original formulation, control theory identified four crucial factors in securing conformity: attachment (to parents, schools, peers), commitment (to conventional behaviour patterns), involvement (in conventional behaviour patterns, and belief (in conventional values). Although Hirschi's work did not engage with girls (indeed, the female component of his sample was subsequently dropped 'remarkably and without explanation': Messerschmidt 1993: 3), the problematic of conformity was taken up in later studies with a specific gender focus.

Hagan (1989) utilized this approach by locating conformity as differentially secured within family structures in western societies. The family, as the primary site for the reproduction of gender roles and identities, is seen by Hagan as tending toward one of two types: the 'patriarchal' and the 'egalitarian'. The 'type' of family is in turn defined by its relationship to the paid employment sector. Hence the 'patriarchal' family in its ideal type would have a male father/husband figure working outside the home, and a mother/wife figure in the home (i.e. not in paid employment); conversely in the 'egalitarian' type both would work in paid employment outside the home. Within the family structure of whatever type, daughters tend to be more controlled by their mothers and tend to greater degrees of conformity. In 'egalitarian' families, however, girls are encouraged more to become risk takers, orienting them toward a future role in the paid production sphere, and the gender differences in socialization diminish. Since risk-taking is in turn related positively to the propensity to become involved in crime, so do gender differences in delinquency diminish in 'egalitarian' families. Girls' conformity in patriarchal families is more readily secured because of the greater controls upon them (Hagan 1989; Messerschmidt 1993: 11–12).

Despite numerous subsequent criticisms for its sexism ('mother's liberation causes daughter's crime', Chesney-Lind 1989: 20, in Messerschmidt 1993: 12), Hagan's work does raise the question of female conformity as an important strand in explaining the gendered character of youth crime.

A directly feminist position is adopted by Heidensohn (1996). Arguing that a feminist approach was 'necessary' to free female crime from its 'invisible state', she comments that, 'paradoxically, an examination of female criminality and unofficial deviance suggests that we need to move away from studying infractions and look at conformity instead, because the most striking thing about female behaviour on the basis of all the evidence considered here is how notably conformist to social mores women are' (Heidensohn 1996: 11). Heidensohn approaches the question of women and control in two general senses, not in themselves incompatible with Hagan's analysis, but treated quite differently. She characterizes these as 'women in control' and 'the control of women'.

Firstly, the sexual division of labour (the gendered apportioning of social roles and tasks in the spheres of familial and paid production) locates women as primary 'controllers'. Through their role in the family – and despite the increasing participation of women in the paid labour market – 'the tasks women are required to carry out to ensure stability in civil society are awesome' (p. 166). In particular,

> While rearing the next generation, women must maintain high (indeed increasingly high) standards of domestic order so that their husbands and children have clean, comfortable refuges to return to from the toil of the day . . . It is also assumed that marriage to a 'good woman' will limit the delinquent proclivities of young men and that, once settled into a situation where he is cared for and occupied a young criminal will mature out of his misdeeds.
>
> (p. 166)

When women do not comply with the ideology of control, they are blamed for increases in public disorder: absent mothers, inadequate mothers, single mothers, working mothers, have all been variously accused of being responsible for the (male) youth crime rate (p. 167). Because of the weight of these societal expectations, Heidensohn argues that women's investment in societal stability is 'clearly enormous'. In other senses, too, women play a significant role in the maintenance of social order. In their roles in the control professions (for example social work and criminal justice occupations) they occupy the position of the 'patriarchal feminine': they have 'been assimilated into the existing patriarchal system as professional handmaidens . . . women are interposed between the state and people, strategically softening the sternness of its power' (p. 173). Women are not typically in positions of high authority in the police force, the prison service, the legal profession or the social work professions, but they control for the controllers.

Women thus have a high stake in conformity due to their responsibilities as controllers; but more, argues Heidensohn, 'this pales beside the complex but enormously limiting forces which operate *upon* women' (p. 174). Women are constrained at home through domestic responsibilities (the famous truism that it is more difficult to commit armed robbery when pushing a baby buggy) through discipline and domination, whether physically and psychologically through domestic violence, or through other forms of subordinating ideologies which frame women as the peacekeepers and the home-makers rather than the breadwinners and the risk-takers. The public nature of much conventional criminality by default means that women, who even in the late twentieth century live far more within the 'private sphere' of home and family than do men, are less likely to participate in 'normal crimes' (Hagan *et al.* 1979; Box 1983). This in turn may be linked to notions of opportunity and differential association (Box 1983), since the sexual division of labour and the ideology of femininity severely limit women's access in particular to more serious forms of crime. Organized crime, for example, 'is not an "equal opportunity employer"; there are glorified Godfathers, but what happened to the Godmothers? They are relegated to subordinate participatory positions' (Box 1983: 182). Similarly, there are so few women in positions of real power within the corporate and financial sectors that they are unlikely to number among the Robert Maxwells of this world (Box 1983; Levi 1994).

Thus the variants of control theory begin to offer possibilities for a broadening of the horizons in youth criminology by highlighting the gendered nature of conformity. A further, related, avenue of inquiry has been to turn attention to the regulation of girls through 'policing'. This term is defined in a much broader sense than that of the police force; rather, it refers to control and containment through the criminal justice system more broadly and through other societal institutions which are implicated in securing conformity among girls and women. As Cain (1989: 1) comments, 'feminist criminologists had begun to point out the continuity between the ways in which women and girls are pressured and schooled to conformity by the criminal justice system and the ways in which they are controlled by a myriad of other institutions and structures in society at large'. The criminal justice system is usually the last domain through which girls are policed because the everyday scrutinies to which they are subjected are far closer than those applied to boys. In this sense feminism *transgresses* criminology because very few girls escape other, 'lower level' forms of control sufficiently to find themselves the object of the scrutiny of the criminal justice system (Hagan *et al.* 1979; Cain 1989). Nevertheless the question remains as to what happens when girls do transcend informal modes of control and become the focus of official attention. Feminist research has suggested that the kinds of concerns – particularly the focus on the sexuality and sexual reputation of girls – which characterize informal controls over them in everyday life (Lees 1989) are reproduced 'writ large' in the criminal justice system. The notion of 'chivalry' suggests that girls are less likely to come to the attention of the courts because of paternalism on the part of police officers, or are treated more leniently when they are brought before the court (see Cavadino and Dignan 1997: 280–3); however, research findings have also suggested that where female offenders are perceived as contravening norms of acceptable feminine behaviour then they may be 'doubly damned': they have broken the formal law, and they have broken the informal rules of femininity. Indeed, in some cases, the very notion of girls having broken the law suggests to the court that (since 'normal' femininity is conformist) there must be something very wrong with these young women. In the latter cases the response of the court is likely to result in greater intervention and more severe sentences than would otherwise be the case (Morris 1987; Heidensohn 1996; Cavadino and Dignan 1997). These are complex issues based on a great deal of often contradictory evidence which it is not the purpose of this chapter to examine in detail; what is of interest is the way in which a focus upon girls as offenders immediately opens up a whole series of new questions which had simply not been considered relevant to traditional criminology.

If girls are offenders, does this mean that there must be something 'special' about them? Why is it not possible to make simple comparisons between the sentencing of boys and girls? The answer to the first question must certainly be that numerically, it is unusual for girls to engage in crime to the same extent as boys; whether this must make them qualitatively 'different' (from what?) is another issue. The answer to the second must tentatively be that certainly the responses of the courts themselves, through the sentencing process, appear to construct female offenders as 'special' and male offenders as 'normal', reinforcing the notion that criminality is a male preserve and that female criminality is a very peculiar phenomenon indeed.

This further highlights the silent spaces in the discipline. What *of* female criminals? Female criminality remains an underresearched area. Studies of female criminals have tended to reflect stereotypes of sex roles by, for example, concentrating on petty female property crime such as shoplifting or prostitution (Morris 1987). This emphasis has been challenged both statistically and theoretically. Morris writes:

In brief, it is questionable how helpful it is to categorize such offences as predominantly 'masculine' or 'feminine' . . . clearly, women are more commonly labelled prostitutes or criminalized in the interaction, but the actual behaviour objected to requires two persons . . . and the female prostitute services a number of male 'clients' . . . More men than women, therefore, are 'involved' in prostitution. Similarly, shoplifting is not numerically more common amongst women and girls than amongst men and boys . . . The claim that shoplifting is an offence committed mainly by women is a myth, but one which persists.

(Morris 1987: 30)

Morris thus objects to an overemphasis on women's conformity and to the sex role-typing of female criminality; she contends that the tendency to socialize women into a certain role may not speak to their criminality or lack of it at all:

Explanations for conformity and criminality can be linked: for example, women may be socialized into a certain kind of role – passive, dependent, gentle and so on – which is far removed from the stereotype of criminality; criminal women, therefore, may also be those who are under- or badly socialized, or who reject that socialization . . . But explanations for conformity and criminal behaviour need not be linked. Women can be socialized in a particular way, but nevertheless commit crimes . . . Criminal behaviour is not peculiar to any particular . . . sex; the same explanatory principles should be relevant for each or at least be able to take account of any differences in criminal behaviour.

(pp. 39–40)

On the basis of this, Morris would argue against a 'special' theory for women's criminality, and calls for a reconsideration of the relevance to women of 'general' criminological theories (p. 75). The problem with this, of course, is whether theories which have been constructed on the basis of male researchers studying the experiences of boys and men *can* be deemed to be general theories. Certainly Leonard (1982), Box (1983) and Messerschmidt (1993) show that there are circumstances in which 'general' (that is, 'malestream') criminological theories as discussed in Chapter 2 of this volume can plausibly be applied to female crime: but equally, one might contend, there are as many circumstances in which they cannot (Messerschmidt 1993). The problem has been the lack of empirical studies which would make these kinds of arguments open to evaluation.

Carlen *et al.*'s *Criminal Women* (1985) was ground-breaking in this respect. Utilizing detailed life histories of criminal women, the authors are able to demonstrate that women who offend express values or objectives which may well be espoused also by male criminals; yet at the same time it is undeniable that their criminal careers are refracted through life experiences which are specifically gendered. Indeed, they are able to use criminal women's accounts (in this case, some of the authors' own) to show that the problem is not so much one of whether crime (or particular crimes) should be conceptualized in terms of 'masculine/feminine', but rather one of the inadvisability of creating any monolithic, monocausal approach to explaining offending:

> The autobiographical accounts demonstrate in fine detail how, under certain material and ideological conditions, either law-breaking and/or other forms of deviant protest may indeed comprise rational and coherent responses to women's awareness of the social disabilities imposed upon them by discriminatory and exploitative class and gender relations. Second, that the complexity of the accounts should call into question *all* of the monocausal and global theories of crime.
>
> (Carlen *et al.* 1985: 8–9)

The women's accounts in Carlen *et al.*'s study show that criminal women may espouse a desire for fun, independence, success; their criminal acts may be intentional and rational within their particular circumstances; and the nature of their criminal activities certainly do not remain tied to shoplifting or prostitution:

> Although their individual quests for success took entirely different forms, each one of them, at some time in her career, deliberately engaged in lawbreaking as a way of either achieving satisfaction as a person or of resolving some of the contradictions facing her as a woman. Chris . . . saw crime as a way of fulfilling her need for excitement and success; Christina . . . on several occasions saw crime as being the best way of achieving her desire for kicks and high income . . . Jenny, a working class woman with an entrepreneurial flair, saw fraud as being the only method by which she could ever expect to succeed as a business woman in a man's world.
>
> (p. 11)

Carlen's achievement in this and subsequent work (see, for example, *Women, Crime and Poverty*, 1988) was to show the importance of debunking either an overreliance on 'grand theory' which denies the complexity of individual experience, or an overreliance on notions of the 'masculine' and the 'feminine', *without* denying that criminality is undoubtedly engaged in and experienced through life experiences which are differentiated by one's positioning in gendered social relations. As such, it shifted the ground of debate away from a simple critique of the 'malestream' but retained the need for a recognition of the gendering of the 'crime question'.

What is still lacking, however, is a body of comparable research with girls who offend. While the bulk of criminological research in the 'formative years' concentrated on young male offenders, and the feminist critique at least re-focused on women offenders and the gendering of crime, most studies of girls have occurred within a broader ambit of youth studies or cultural studies (McRobbie and Nava 1984; McRobbie 1991). 'Girlhood' has been researched largely within a concern with 'bedroom cultures', the everyday interactions of young female social networks, sexuality, or the dynamics of consumption (for example of fashion, magazines, music and advertising: Förnas and Bolin 1995). Similarly there are many studies of the ways in which girls are processed by the welfare and criminal justice systems, focusing in particular on the sexualization of their offending (see discussion above, and Hudson 1989). A further area has been the feminist contribution to the study of women and girls as victims of crime (see Chapter 5), which while of undisputed importance, still does not address the question of the girl offender. Where studies of girls' criminality have occurred, they have usually focused on issues of drug use, prostitution, or girls' participation in gangs (Campbell 1984; Cain 1989).

Since empirical knowledge of girl offenders is so limited compared to studies of boys, it is very difficult to achieve any finer-grained understanding of the gendering of youthful criminality, and much easier to concentrate on girls' *lack* of criminality on the one hand and boys' crime-*proneness* on the other. The latter are the focus of the latest 'knowledge explosion' occuring within criminology, taking us back to boys through masculinities theories.

Boy-ness and crime: masculinities

The very positioning of boys within criminology as the 'typical' offender has obscured one glaring factor: if it is to be boys who occupy the criminological gaze, then surely their 'boy-ness' ought at least to be an issue? Notwithstanding the references within many of the formative studies (and particularly those of the Centre for Contemporary Cultural Studies) towards masculinity, it has only been recently that masculinity (or, the preferred term, masculini*ties*) has begun to emerge as a growth industry within criminology (Newburn and Stanko 1994). As Messerschmidt notes,

> There is little doubt that, although traditionally written by men and primarily about men and boys, major theoretical works in criminology are alarmingly gender-blind. That is, while men and boys have been seen as the 'normal subjects', the gendered content of their legitimate and illegitimate behaviour has been virtually ignored. So remarkable has been the gender-blindness of criminology that whenever the high gender ratio of crime is actually considered, criminology has asked 'why is it that women do not offend'? (rather than 'why do men disproportionately commit crime'?) . . .
>
> (Messerschmidt 1993: 1)

The message to be taken from this is that somehow masculinity is bound up with criminality, and masculinities theory is a necessary precursor to an understanding of how this might be so. We must therefore consider masculinities as an area of study in general before considering how it might be applied to criminological understandings of gender divisions in youth crime. As with feminist theories (and partly stemming from or through engagement with such theories), masculinities theories question fundamentally the innateness of sex role differences. 'To be a man', as 'to be a woman', is not something which is biologically given, but something which is achieved through social practices. Predicated on a complex analysis of historical developments in the division of labour in society, we can but summarize this briefly here (see Messerschmidt 1993: Chapter 3). As Heidensohn (1996) related female conformity to women's positioning in the structures of the gendered division of labour, so Messerschmidt notes that in western societies, 'labor has been divided by gender for (1) housework (2) child care (3) unpaid versus paid work, and (4) within the paid labor market and individual workplaces' (1993: 64). This division of labour entails considerable inequalities of power and authority between men and women:

> A manifestation of gender relations of power is the obvious structural fact that men control the economic, religious, political, and military institutions of authority and coercion in society. In addition to such large-scale institutional power, gender power organizes advantage and inequality within smaller social groups and institutions (e.g., the family, peer group, and workplace) . . . in most (but clearly not all) situations, men are able to impose authority, control, and coercion over women.
>
> (Messerschmidt 1993: 71; see also Connell 1987)

Masculinities, however, operate within hierarchies which are not simply based on a male–female dichotomy, but on the notion of hierarchies of power which delineate 'more' and 'less' masculine men. It is important to appreciate that when Messerschmidt talks of 'gender power', he is not characterizing power as a 'thing' which men simply have over women. The whole point about the gender division of labour is that it arranges individuals in relation to other individuals (Messerschmidt 1993: 71). This can include men over men, and also is not dependent upon one source of power such as access to material resources. A woman may have more access to material resources than an unemployed man, but it does not necessarily decrease his interpersonal power in terms of his ability to rape (p. 72). Also,'power among men is likewise unequally distributed since some groups of men (in terms of class, race, and sexual preference, for instance) have greater authority and, therefore, more power than others' (p. 72, citing Connell 1987). Some men, in other words, are more manly than others; some women are more able to resist male subordination than others. The 'ultimate masculinity' reigns both above other men and above other women, in terms of numerous constellations of prowess: cultural dominance, access to material resources, physical force (or the ability to command physical force), and so on.

Unlike (for the most part) early feminist theories of the masculine–feminine relationship, masculinities theories tend to emphasize the notion of hegemonic and subordinated masculinities. This is really to acknowledge the hierarchization of gender/power relations. Referring back to Chapters 2 and 3, this is based on the notion of Gramscian Marxism that hegemony is a dominant conception of reality diffused throughout social life and which 'comprises "the 'spontaneous' consent given by the great masses of the population to the general direction imposed on social life by the dominant fundamental group"' (Messerschmidt 1993: 81–2, citing Gramsci 1978).

The question is, what does this actually *mean*? Messerschmidt argues that 'simply defined, in any culture, hegemonic masculinity is the idealized form of masculinity in a given historical setting. It is culturally honored, glorified, and extolled' (p. 82, following Connell 1987).

Quite who, or what, the 'dominant fundamental group' are may leave one somewhat perplexed; but the general point that a consensus operates in society to sustain notions of idealized masculinity can hardly be misunderstood once the male fantasy figures in sport and popular culture are considered, nor that these notions contain embedded within them connotations of power which may not be easy to articulate or precisely pin down yet are nevertheless strangely tangible. Subordinated masculinities, then, must represent those forms of masculinity which express a different voice, such as male gay culture. This leads to the idea that 'masculinity' (and hence the term masculini*ties*) is a contested ground – to state the obvious! *Men* cannot agree about what masculinity is, but some have more power than others to make their voices heard.

Messerschmidt argues that hegemonic masculinity is

> defined through work in the paid-labor market, the subordination of women, heterosexism, and the driven and uncontrollable sexuality of men. Refined still further, hegemonic masculinity emphasizes practices toward authority, control, competitive individualism, independence, aggressiveness, and the capacity for violence.
>
> (Messerschmidt 1993: 82)

The qualities of subordinated masculinities receive rather less attention: gay cool? the male victim? the ecological tree dwelling/tunnel digging male?

It is further possible (and probably likely) that these rather general sociological treatments of masculinities can go only so far. This is simply because, having stressed that there is a relationship between what is ascribed (hierarchies of material resources, physical power) and what is achieved (the identity of who I am/want to be), masculinities studies hit a central problem: how is masculinity achieved subjectively? Put in its simplest form: if you are a male and you are a football fan: why? (Hornby 1992). Hegemonic masculinity as embodied in football culture denotes not only physical prowess, wealth, sexual power, but also a form of assertion of the desirable way to *be* which locks out femininity by default. No matter how many women watch or even play football, they are ultimately there as spectators to the psychic structure, the 'deep play', in which only masculinity matters (Williams and Taylor 1994: 214).

Jefferson (1994) argues for the need to theorize masculine subjectivity in order to begin to understand how masculinities take expression in culture. Boys and men do not simply assimilate the hegemonic ideal of masculinity unproblematically; some reject it (as through some forms of gay culture), and others adopt an approximation to it, but not without experiencing a good deal of pain along the way. Hegemonic masculinity, indeed, while offering the 'advantages' of power over others, creates a good deal of insecurity for boys and men:

> I have argued that the idea of masculinity as an ideal that all men aspire to and which is unproblematically internalised by successive generations of male children . . . ignores the obvious difficulties that boys and men often have in either accepting or achieving the ideal, or both. This all but universal experience of failure can lead to an active rejection of the ideal on offer and a positive identification with an alternative, albeit subordinate, masculinity; painful, sometimes frenzied, attempts to drag an unwilling psyche into line with the unwanted social expectations; living a quiet life of desperation; or, perhaps most commonly, a lot of faking it.
>
> (Jefferson 1994: 13)

What then, do these explorations in masculinity imply for the study of youth and crime? Certainly, that if we return to the question of the 'boyness' of crime as a problematic, then it is the relationship between attempts to achieve masculinity, the practices implied by that, and the subjective orientations required for it, which must be placed centre stage in understanding a whole range of male criminal behaviour. It is not too difficult to see how many earlier studies of, for example, boys in gangs or groups show how they become involved in delinquency as a way of 'doing masculinity'. Most of the studies discussed in Chapter 2 can be re-theorized in this way. The 'frustrated aspirations' mode of explanation so often used in early theorizing can be framed as frustrated (masculine) aspirations, as Messerschmidt's reworking of some of this literature demonstrates (Messerschmidt 1994). Aggressive normative heterosexuality, power over young women, toughness, smartness, group territorialism, individual competitiveness, and other attributes of delinquency in (male) group settings may be understood as ways of aspiring to hegemonic masculinity; if legitimate avenues are unavailable or unattainable then illegitimate ones are usually attainable. Referring back to Willis's 'Lads' and 'Ear'oles' in *Learning to Labour* (1977), Messerschmidt situates the oppositional behaviour of 'the Lads' specifically within masculinity:

> The Lads come to school armed with traditional notions of white, working class masculinity: the idea that 'real men' choose manual, not mental labour . . . schooling is deemed irrelevant to their working class future and 'emasculating' to their conception of masculinity . . . Constructing masculinity around physical aggression, the Lads – eschewing academic achievement – draw on an available resource that allows them to distance and differentiate themselves from the non-violent 'Ear'oles . . . Such behaviours help transcend the 'sissyish' quality of the school day while simultaneously distancing the Lads from the conformists.
>
> (Messerschmidt 1994: 92–3)

Masculinity, then, will be done differently in different settings and according to different cultural resources available: sometimes this will fall on the wrong side of the law. Hence Levi, discussing the relationship of masculinity to white-collar crime, argues that the values of deregulated corporate capitalism are themselves highly masculinist, which provides a cultural resource in which fraud becomes a kind of overdrive version of 'normal practice':

> Many [convicted fraudsters] are 'driven' characters for whom, in the words of Gordon Gekko in *Wall Street*, 'lunch is for wimps' and everything is subordinated to the objectives of attaining peer-group respect, of controlling others and avoiding being controlled by them. It may also be that despite the apparent gender-neutrality of 'deceitfulness' that is at the core of fraud, men are prone to adopt an 'aggressive' rather than 'compliant' style of manipulativeness. It may be no accident that mega-salespeople in financial services attract the *soubriquet* 'Big Swinging Dick': I know of no women who have been awarded that honorary title!
>
> (Levi 1994: 250)

Again, Campbell, in a more journalistic account (1993), uses a kind of masculinity theory to account for the activities of young men in episodes of urban unrest. Dispossessed young males in tracts of urban wasteland, deprived of their 'traditional' modes of doing masculinity (the breadwinner, the patriarch, the head of household) instead find alternative resources in the cultures of wrecking and joyriding (see Chapter 3). While the women

attempt to deal with the problems of long-term urban decline through com-
munitarian solutions, attempting to 'build up' fragmented structures
through credit unions, local self-help schemes and working with the local
authorities, the boys concentrate on smashing things up:

> The men and boys arraigned in Cardiff's riot trials would, in the olden
> days of the Fifties and Sixties, when their parents were their age, have
> been wrought in the image of what used to be known as 'the working
> man' . . . One generation later the men's relationship to the world of
> work has changed: instead of being defined by work, it came increas-
> ingly to be defined by crime.
>
> (Campbell 1993: 196)

For Campbell, this response through crime to a loss of traditional masculinity is not simply rational and material (an income by other means), but
ingrained more deeply in 'macho' subjectivity. Hence, for example, her
depiction of the joyriding culture:

> The driver was dressed, the car was ready . . . the hooded driver, known
> as the Don, revved a stolen two-litre Maestro and skated past the
> police and a watching crowd at 60 mph . . . This master of joyriding
> did indeed bring great joy to his audience, who savoured the chagrin of
> the officers doomed to do nothing but watch man tango with machine.
> Rude and red, the Maestro was a perfect dancing partner for the mys-
> tery man . . . 'That was to show that we ain't skinning teeth, we're not
> fucking around, we're doing what we want!' explained the Don.
>
> (Campbell 1993: 254)

Thus in one sense, emergent writings on masculinities and crime are
beginning to attempt what Carlen set out to do for 'women and crime' in
Criminal Women (1985) over a decade ago: gender and gendered practices
may be seen as a prism through which acts, sometimes criminal, are
refracted. Crime is not presented as reducible to masculinity, nor is masculinity seen as a unity; but there, running through much criminal activity,
are social practices which frequently are positioned, in various ways,
toward the cultural predominance of the hegemonic masculine ideal. Much
of this work to date has concerned itself with re-evaluating the mass of previous 'malestream' criminology. But there is a problem here, in that com-
paratively few studies are as yet available which specifically built
masculinities theory into their original conceptualization (*British Journal
of Criminology* 1988); and there are many areas yet to be explored, such as
the emergent literature on subordinated masculinities: what happens, for
example, when boys or men are victims? What of boys' fear of crime? Boys,
after all, are not just offenders (Newburn and Stanko 1994; Goodey 1995).
The contribution of masculinities theorizing in criminology is very much
an unfinished story, albeit one of interest and promise.

Beyond the boy zone?

Clearly the work on gender and crime discussed in this chapter does prise open a little more the vice-like grip which 'youth crime equals male offender' has exerted on the field of youth criminology. It takes us beyond the 'boy zone': but how far?

While many of the recent studies of gender and crime have emphasized the multiple, flexible and achieved nature of gendered practices, thereby rendering gender irreducible to 'crime' or vice versa, perhaps there are difficulties in treating the domain of the 'criminal' as always-already gendered. From a conventional wisdom in early criminology in which gender was virtually ignored, there is a danger in the 'new' gendered criminology of producing a conventional wisdom in which gender *cannot* be ignored, since its importance is so 'obvious'. Is 'gender' always useful in understanding youth criminality, youth victimization or youth justice policy? Does masculinities theory return us too glibly to the boy zone? In beginning to recognize the diversity of both crime (it is not just about the everyday crimes of the young and poor) and gender (it is not just about unitary identities of male and female), criminology may ultimately have to question the relevance of giving either youthfulness or gender too much centrality in understanding crime.

Further reading

Heidensohn (1994) provides an overview of the study of female criminality in criminology, and an application of control theory to gender and crime (1996). Box (1983: Chapter 5) remains a relevant discussion of female powerlessness and crime. Carlen is an unmissable author on gender and criminality (Carlen *et al.* 1985, Carlen 1988 for example). Leonard (1982) provides a useful early reassessment of 'malestream' criminology, and Messerschmidt (1993) also gives a critique and reassessment of conventional theorizing in the light of 'masculinities'. Newburn and Stanko (1994) provide an interesting edited collection on aspects of masculinities and crime. Jefferson, in the 1997 edition of the *Oxford Handbook of Criminology* (Maguire *et al.* 1997), demonstrates an application of psychoanalytic perspectives to masculinities and crime.

chapter seven

Conclusion: listening to youth?

Revisiting the domains of youth and crime: discarding the comfort blanket
Disparate histories, enduring themes: the powers of articulation

In this chapter we summarize the arguments presented in the preceding six chapters, not simply as an aid to memory for the dazed and confused, but with a wider purpose in view. We have attempted, through a presentation of some of the central ways in which 'youth and crime' has been constructed in the popular, policy and academic worlds, to indicate the problems which arise once the shackles of 'what we all know' are discarded. At the same time, this can be a discomfiting experience. How do these different insights into different worlds fit together to provide us with an 'answer' about youth and crime? What is it we are supposed to 'know', or 'believe', at the end of it all? The field of 'youth and crime' has been presented as one which shifts according to the perspective taken upon it; that perspective, in turn, shifts with history, culture, economic and political circumstances, institutional interests and priorities. Some of these twists and turns in perspective appear to operate at the broadest level of collective consciousness, others at the micro level of individual interest, and at many levels in between. The chapters appear as a series of 'domains': territories of knowledge which belong to no single individual or social grouping, but which nevertheless, at different times and in different ways, seem to produce distinctive tendencies. The task of this chapter is to briefly revisit each domain, and then to consider whether we can identify, if not unifying threads, at least some enduring themes. Last but not least, we address some of the deliberate absences in our own textual treatment of youth and crime, and consider some potential future directions for 'understanding'.

Revisiting the domains of youth and crime: discarding the comfort blanket

It is, then, comforting to think that the 'youth crime problem' is an obvious one. Surely most crimes are committed by young people, therefore the answer is to explain why, and to do something about it? The astute reader will have noticed that we do not, in fact, address either of these apparently central issues in the text. Instead, we have chosen to focus upon the way in which the 'youth crime problem' became seen in this light, and to highlight other possible ways of seeing which seem to have got lost in the obsession with the youthful offender and his (*sic*) punishment. The relatively disparate domains which we confront in the separate chapters can, in fact, be re-presented as a fairly coherent narrative of the historical articulation of one version of a 'problem' and the corresponding lack of articulation of other possible 'problems'. This section revisits our earlier chapters in this light.

Age as a social category, and childhood and youth as 'other'

This may be considered the prehistory of youth and crime. Without particular conceptions of childhood and youth, we would have no question to address. While the cultural and historical variability of the definitions of crime have become a staple issue within criminology and sociology, less attention has been paid to the definitions of childhood and youth. This prehistory is important, not for the sake of mere pedantry, but because historically specific conditions produced our taken-for-granted assumptions that childhood and youth are 'given' states of human development. It forms the basis for a framing of the youth crime question throughout the twentieth century, which has largely taken for granted the dependency of childhood and the troublesomeness of youth. It also forms the basis for assumptions about the respectability of middle age and the vulnerability of old age. Quite tangible results occurred as a result of this prehistory: most notably an ever ready eagerness to project the troubles of any given era on to the state of youth as some kind of barometer of the general health of society, and a concomitant reluctance to admit the destructive or criminogenic tendencies of the middle aged and elderly. Childhood and youth – productions of adult desires and longings – were made to represent the dichotomy of the hopes and fears of nation: a quite impossible role for the marginalized to fulfil.

Enter criminology: science and objectivity?

It is then hardly surprising that criminology – as an eclectic disciplinary field with one foot in academia and one in the regulatory concerns of the state – should have, from its inception, focused overwhelmingly on youth and crime. Throughout the formative decades of the 1920s to the 1970s criminology in its various guises reflected and reinforced 'official' (and popular) concerns with youth-as-problem. 'Youth and the health of the nation' remained very much related to criminological and sociological concerns well into the period of post-Second World War reconstruction. This stemmed partly from the institutional contexts within which these disciplines developed in a transatlantic interchange, and partly from the internal dynamics of their academic concerns. Despite the limited challenges of radical and critical criminologies in the 1960s and 1970s, the centrality of the 'youth problem' to criminological knowledge was never to be transcended. In academic discourse as elsewhere, 'crime' continued to imply youth, and 'youth' to imply crime. Young people were to remain the problematized and the criminalized and – with the exception of radical cultural studies – youth criminology (in effect) the handmaiden of official and popular concern. The voices of young people themselves were rarely heard, and then only through the more-or-less elaborate reconstructions of their lives presented by (adult male) academics. 'Scientific' and 'objective' social inquiries for the large part accepted the foundations laid down in prehistory unproblematically.

I read the news today: youth crime and the popular media

Our third domain is that of 'popular' representation. Increasingly, academic criminology operates in relation to media and popular cultural constructions of youth and crime. The proliferation of popular media in the electronic, globalized era comes to form a most important context for understandings of youth and crime. Through the complex processes of the production and consumption of cultural images, a hegemonic constellation of everyday knowledges has emerged. From specific 'moral panics' surrounding young people not dissimilar to those seen in our prehistory domain, through the 1970s to the 1990s, ever more reciprocal relationships between the media, the political and the populace fostered an explosion of panic concerning the young. Qualitatively and quantitatively more pervasive, the new wave of media representation first generalized, and then totalized, the assumed relationship between young people, crime and the state of society. Tied into escalating anxieties over the collapse of the welfare state and late modern capitalism, the youth 'crisis' reached fever pitch. Adult worries over everything from unemployment to consumer boom, urban degeneration to video nasties, were to find expression in a lament for the lost generation. Again there was nothing intrinsically new that was not there in embryo in the prehistory, but by the 1990s it had dispersed into every corner of everyday life; the distinction between 'factual' and 'fictive' categories had collapsed as surely as the distinction between direct and mediated experience. It had become ever more difficult to frame 'youth' outside 'crime'.

The comforting pragmatics of policy?

The policy domain should surely provide refuge for those who do not wish to engage with the discomfiting relativities of cultural analysis. For surely policy is about pragmatics, finding the most effective solutions to practical social problems? Yet in the tortuous twists and turns of criminal justice policy, children and young people have been subject to 'care' and 'control', 'treatment' and 'punishment'. Lying behind all of the policy provisions of the twentieth century have been the strategies of politicians, criminal justice agents and agencies to harness young people in the regulation of society through moral (and thereby cultural) languages. Whether stemming from good intentions (such as philanthropic concern), naked self-interest (winning adult votes), the pragmatics of governance (controlling public spending) or the desire for the maintenance and strengthening of hierarchies of existing power (authoritarianism), 'youth' has been dragged along by adult institutions in their quest to secure a complex web of political interests. The young have been constructed through policy not as citizens, but as objects of increasingly repressive modes of governance. As adult anxiety and punitive desire escalate, the (metaphorical) body of the delinquent is carved up to serve political and popular appetites, and effectiveness and rationality are increasingly subsumed under ideological imperative.

Out of sight: young people as victims

If young people have been selectively constructed as 'problem' and 'other'; if their concerns have been marginalized, their lifestyles problematized and their voices subdued, what has been lost in our understanding of youth and crime? One largely neglected set of issues relates to the unpopular notion of children and young people as victims of crime. Because the idea of the 'victim' connotes blamelessness, it is very difficult to conceptualize young people in this way. Except in conjunction with the ideology of childhood 'innocence' – itself increasingly shaken by the demonization of ever younger age groups – the predominant categorizations of youth do not sit easily within a 'victim' discourse. 'True victims' – except for child victims of random killers or sex attackers – are culturally reserved spaces for the infantilized elderly. The idea of young people as victims of social or legal injustice, as victims of widespread incidences of assault within institutional contexts (whether the family, the school, or residential state institutions), or as victims of everyday crimes in public space: these are areas of relative silence. Only recently has criminology itself begun to challenge these omissions in any concerted fashion, and in popular and policy discourse such issues are often treated with cynicism, disdain or vehement denial. Indeed, it is possible to argue that this is a symptom of society in denial, a society so attached to a psychic need to project fears and failures onto the young that it is afraid to acknowledge the scale of adult crimes against them.

Gender and beyond: challenging youth and crime

The idea of youth victimization raises important questions about subjugated or denied knowledges. However refracted through other formations such as class and race, it is the dyad of (male) youth and (criminal) youth which above all characterizes any vision of what it means to understand youth and crime. Thus although subconscious ideas of race and class also impinge, youth is fearfully personified within the popular psyche as *male* and *criminal*. Criminology has only recently begun to deconstruct this conflation, helped by the gender-based analysis of the last two decades. Perhaps then it is not so much 'youthfulness' as 'masculinities' which are at issue; perhaps not so much 'offending' as 'victimization'? This is not to suggest simply replacing one exclusionary set of obsessions with another. It is to suggest that the framing of the 'youth crime problem' as 'the crime problem' – however comprehensible as a historical and cultural phenomenon – has created a kind of subsidence in the foundations of understanding crime which will not be easily amenable to quick repair.

Disparate histories, enduring themes: the powers of articulation

If there is one overarching theme of this text, it is that the 'youth crime problem' as it has conventionally been approached is neither more nor less than a product. It is not a product of absent fathers or single mothers, nor a product of unemployment or lack of discipline, but a product of the production and consumption of knowledges.

To avert the outrage of realists, and to avoid as far as possible the sin of contributing to the aetiological crisis, it is important here to insert a timely caveat. Careful empirical analysis has (and will continue to) show distinct correlations between specific social circumstances, specific personality traits, specific situational dynamics and the commission of specific criminal acts. Since the commission of these acts is not only real, but real in its effects, we have no desire to take refuge in cultural relativism in the sense of attempting to wave away crime (whether committed by young people or not) as being merely linguistic or definitional. Nor are we assuming a comparable moral relativism in relation to the sanctioning and control of acts which are deleterious to social well-being. What this text has endeavoured to demonstrate is that the framing of the 'youth crime problem' in particular ways has produced specific ways of seeing and responding to youth and crime which are also real in their effects.

If we are to be 'realist' about the crimes *of* young people, why are we not equally realist about crimes and social injustices *against* young people? In the end, the answer lies within the powers of articulation. Since the young are a marginal category (or a constellation of marginal categories, if preferred, refracted through other social positionings and hierarchies of power), they are non-persons. Since they are non-persons, they are outside of claims to citizenship. Since they are not enfranchised, they stand outside of formal polity. Their 'powers' are inarticulated and thereby accorded qualities of danger without reference to the voices of young people themselves.

Policy-makers, academics, the popular media and politicians still speak as if there were an obvious 'community' – which young people as non-citizens stand outside – whose interests can be identified and operationalized and set against the 'enemy' (the marginal groups) in the form of practical strategies (of, for example, punishment, or crime prevention). A study of the notion of 'community' or 'society', however, quickly reveals that the concept typically operates to obfuscate ideological and material divisions in social life and obscure the interests on which they are based (Thorpe 1985). Power operates in relation to the life course to produce 'youth' as the problematic section of the population to which 'community' or 'society' must address itself in order to protect itself from crime and disorder. Yet 'safety' for some is secured at the cost of silencing others. Policy-makers and academics alike 'represent' not 'community' but their own aspirations and the organizational conventions of the institutions within which they daily work. Excluded from the voice of 'community' or 'society', children and young people occupy a discursive domain foregrounded by popular images of trouble-making, rioting, incivility and rebellion. Much academic endeavour has focused on the same preoccupations as popular discourse with youth as a 'threat' to social order. Psychological and biological languages have in parallel fashion represented young people within a developmental cycle of troublesomeness, turbulence and hormonal anarchy. The gendered character of these discourses has exacerbated these tendencies. Young people are largely excluded from the languages of human rights, legal rights and formal political enfranchisement; they are increasingly marginal to the waged labour force. Even their centrality to the consumer lifestyle market of popular culture has been defined negatively rather than creatively. The cultural and political investment in the production, silencing and scapegoating of the marginal usually ensures their continued marginality; while subordinated voices come to recognize and enjoy their 'dangerousness', which itself becomes a creative force for the reproduction of marginality.

The reframing of 'understanding youth and crime' requires either a dissolution of 'youth' as a special object of knowledge and policy, or an inclusion of young people in the social enterprise through the legitimation of their voices and a recognition of their potential for citizenship. As yet there is very little recognition of this problem in any of the ways in which adults speak of youth and crime. The processes of critical excavation, however, may at least provide us with a starting point for debate. Of all the current enterprises engaged in by criminologists, youth criminology perhaps remains the field most trapped by its past and most confounded by uncritical presupposition. It is hard to leave behind the comfort blanket.

Glossary

Aetiology   In criminology, the notion of the causality of crime. In a critique of 'Left idealist' criminology, proponents of Left realism have claimed that criminology has encountered an 'aetiological crisis' whereby the discipline has lost sight of a concern with crime causation (Young 1994).

Archaeology   As used in social science or cultural analysis, the excavation of layers of knowledge by a process of 'peeling' back layers of discourse and belief rather like the skins of an onion to reveal the historical and cultural organization of a society.

Biologism   A form of reductionism which seeks to explain human characteristics and behaviours in terms of underlying biological factors such as genetic composition. It is often used to challenge critical analyses which emphasize the role of cultural values in shaping personality and behaviour.

Cultural construction   The process by which discourses are produced and sustained within any particular culture by the dominance of certain beliefs and practices.

Cultural transmission theory   The notion that norms and values are passed on through peer group, familial groups, or territory-based groups, so that one's form of association with others is the locus of the reproduction of culture.

Darwinian   Named after Charles Darwin, a theory based on the concept of natural selection, whereby species evolve to best enable them to survive in changing environments, and the strongest and most adaptable species will survive and develop into higher forms as others die out.

Deconstruction   A method or process by which the taken-for-granted nature of representation is questioned, particularly by examining the interests which particular types of representation serve, or their role in upholding certain cultural practices and beliefs. Deconstruction reveals the ideologies which inhere within representations.

Delinquency   Coleman and Moynihan (1996) define delinquency as 'law violations (usually of juveniles)', but the term is sometimes used more loosely to refer to any kind of youthful misconduct. In the USA, 'status offences' are those acts which are offences only if committed by a person within a certain age category' (p. 146). More broadly, one might add that delinquency implies the notion of a 'fallen' or 'subterranean' character.

Deviancy amplification A description of a process whereby societal reaction to deviance indirectly exacerbates the level of deviance, in particular the ways in which the reaction of official agencies of control (the police, the courts, politicians) and the popular media produce a heightened sensitivity toward certain forms of deviance, render people committing those deviant acts more likely to apprehension, and make people more likely to see themselves as deviant and further reinforce their deviant identity.

Discourse A much debated term within social sciences and humanities. It typically involves a notion of a series of related beliefs and values articulated through language. It is often used on the basis that discourse is by its nature public.

Domain A term used in this volume to denote a bounded space of culture and practice: for example, the family domain, the policy domain, the media domain.

Ecology A method of inquiry which stresses the need to map a system (whether biological or social), specifying the precise operation of its component parts and the relationships between them. Using an organic metaphor, it is assumed that ecological systems are essentially self-regulating, different forms of adaptation occurring as component parts interact with each other. It is a social science application particularly in the work of Chicago School sociology, where the ecology of the city is the object of inquiry.

Empirical science A form of scientific practice which stresses the importance of experimentation and practical application of scientific principles. It is particularly central in the development of Victorian industrialism in Britain.

Ethnography A method of study which emphasizes qualitative observation and the immersion of the researcher in the 'field' – i.e. the society or subsection of society being studied. The ethnographer deliberately sets out to 'climb into the shoes of other people and walk around in them'. The assumption is that it is not possible to understand society fully without collapsing the distinction between researcher and researched. Both the researcher's own personal biography, and the biographies of the researched, must be taken into account.

Hegemonic ideology 'Hegemony' in this instance is a term used by Antonio Gramsci (Gramsci 1978). It entails the notion that systems of economic and political power differentiation are maintained because the belief systems which reinforce the interests of the powerful appear to the individual as powerful and taken-for-granted 'truths', even though they may operate to secure the continued disadvantage or oppression of that individual.

Interactionism A methodological and theoretical position based on the notion that meanings are only created as people act and react towards each other. A deviant act, for example, only becomes deviant when it is reacted to as such by others. An act itself has no inherent meaning; such meaning has to be actively constructed as actors negotiate with each other in specific social settings. Similarly a criminal statistic is a product of a series of interactions, rather than an objective measurement of reality.

Justice approach (in juvenile justice) Based on a critique of welfarism which, the proponents of the justice model argued, resulted in the collapse of due process and unjustifiable levels of intervention in the lives of children and their families. Re-emphasized (in the 1980s) the importance of legal process and rights, and proportionality in sentencing rather than unbridled discretion.

Left realism Sometimes referred to as 'radical realism', Left realism is based on a critique of constructionist criminology's emphasis on the role of the state, the law and the mass media in constructing notions of criminality which disadvantage the poor, young people and ethnic minorities. In emphasizing the notion of crime as a social and ideological construct, argue the realists, criminologists have failed in their duty to 'take crime seriously'. Crime is real in its effects, from the Left realist perspective; fear of crime is rational not irrational; and very often it is the poor and the young who are the perpetrators of those offences which disproportionately affect the poor, whose quality of life is already low. It must be seen in the context of its proponents' research activities, which developed local crime surveys in association with local authorities as a means of mapping patterns of victimization and policing practices. It also emphasizes the role of police accountability in democratic societies (Young 1997). It stems in part from the inspiration of feminist criminologists concerned with putting violence and sexual assault against women on the criminological agenda (Heidensohn 1996).

Masculinities   Usually now used in the plural to denote the diversity of masculine subjectivity. A growth area in criminology, 'masculinities' theory emphasizes the achievement and management of self-identity and the social constraints upon the formation of identity. In particular, masculinities theory attempts to explain the relationship between the subjective inner self and the public outer self, and the importance of this for understanding different forms of criminality, such as 'joyriding' or white-collar crime (Newburn and Stanko 1994). 'Hegemonic masculinity' is seen as a particular form of 'doing' manhood which can be damaging to the individual and criminogenic in its consequences.

Medicalization   Related to biologism insofar as it refers to the use of scientific knowledge to explain behaviour. The practical implication is, for example, that if delinquency may be seen as a disease, then it may be treated and 'cured', for example through drug therapy. It also implies that if a person is 'sick', then any curative methods can be justified, and therefore can be denied the rights accorded to 'healthy' people.

Metaphorical   The sense in which language is symbolically laden to express far more than a simple description of the 'real'. Language is always imagery and redolent of culture: for example we feel 'up' or 'down', things cannot be reduced to 'black and white'. Any word, however apparently descriptive, relies on a whole system of shared meanings and assumptions, and is often emotionally laden: for example the description of young offenders as 'animals' dragging society 'down'. Metaphorical analysis can therefore be used to help deconstruct social discourse.

New criminology   The early 1970s in the UK saw the emergence of 'new criminology' or 'critical criminology', which, although drawing upon new deviancy, went further by insisting upon the need to place the study of deviance within a Marxist economic and political framework. The law was to be treated as a tool of the ruling class, and definitions of crime questioned insofar as they served these interests and so perpetuated capitalist oppression. Deviant acts themselves could be seen as rational forms of rebellion against oppression, and criminology should have a socialist agenda which insisted on the importance of eradicating economic exploitation. It is most closely associated with Ian Taylor, Paul Walton and Jock Young (the last – in an interesting turn of events – was later to become the prime advocate of Left realism).

New deviancy theory   A critique of orthodox sociology of delinquency originating in the US in the 1950s and 1960s. Based theoretically around interactionism, 'new deviancy' focused on definitional issues (who defines whom as deviant? how? how is it possible that for some the deviant label sticks, and for others it does not? what kind of social interactions and settings frame the definition of some as deviant and others as not?). Similarly, the world of the social actor was to be taken seriously, and actors' own accounts of deviant motivations given credence. Strongly associated with the work of Matza and Sykes and Howard Becker, New deviancy was subsequently to provide inspiration for radical criminology in Britain (see Chapter 2).

Paradigm   A general framework of knowledge, or an orientation toward the study of natural or social phenomena which shares common features despite the differences within it, and whose general features are systematically related to each other in some way: for example, the 'scientific paradigm'. 'Paradigm shifts' are said to occur when a major or fundamental change in the basis of knowledge and understanding occurs, usually implying philosophical shifts underpinning the way of seeing embraced by the paradigm.

Pathology   A pathological approach to crime suggests that there is an inherent organic malfunction within the offender which causes the offending behaviour. As with medicalization, it takes not only responsibility away from the actor, but also civil rights.

Patriarchy   Again, a much debated term, literally meaning 'the rule of the father'. It refers to the systematic ordering of gender relationships into hierarchies whereby the masculine controls the feminine through the appropriation of material and cultural resources including money, political power, language and knowledge. It is not, however, simply a system in which men control or oppress women; it is a system in which masculinity is the dominant cultural form, and through which men also control other men.

Positivism   A methodological position within the social sciences which assumes that criminals are demonstrably different from non-criminals, and that causative factors within the individual or their life circumstances may be identified and quantified. Positivism may be either biological, psychological or sociological. The methods of empirical science are stressed: quantification, experimentation, statistical correlation and prediction.

Postwar reconstruction   In this volume this term refers to the period after the Second World War and the attempts to rebuild the economic and social infrastructure of the UK, in particular the development of a welfare state under Beveridge and programmes for the expansion of the public education system.

Realism   see Left realism

Representation   A term with a specific meaning in the sociology of knowledge, cultural studies and similar fields. It assumes that knowledge is never unmediated by cultural values and beliefs. Although 'reality' is 'out there', it can never be truly or objectively described. Thus for example the representation of childhood relates to something real (a chronologically young person) but the notion of what constitutes childhood varies from culture to culture and over historical time. Indeed, some cultures would not recognize the term at all. Representations may be produced through the media, through public policies, in popular culture – indeed, through all aspects of social life – and may be produced through language or image.

Stereotype   A schematic portrayal, usually of a 'type' of person, which produces a generalized image (e.g. a 'thug') which plays down individual difference between people and scales up a small number of (usually undesirable) attributes. It is often used pejoratively and in a dehumanizing way to demonize certain groups in society.

Subcultural theory   A perspective concerned with the culture and behaviour of subsets of groups within societies. There are several different strands of subcultural theory but all have in common the notion that there are distinct and identifiable smaller groupings within wider society who share particular values and focal concerns specific to them, as well as values and beliefs of wider society. It is used to explain youth crime and delinquency in terms of the resistances and oppositions towards the parent culture generated, for example, among economically disadvantaged males in authority settings such as the school. Radical subcultural theory, as with the Centre for Contemporary Cultural studies at the University of Birmingham in the 1970s, emphasizes the symbolic importance of subcultures in creating a sense of belonging and community, and the deep meaning of subcultural forms (such as music, dress, sport fandom): what you see is not what you get, hence skinhead culture may be 'read' as the magical recovery of community.

Universalizing discourse   A process by which individual differences are subsumed under a powerful generic definition which is assumed to apply across a population irrespective of any dissimilarities. It has the effect of making a particular notion seem natural or 'common sense', hence the universalization of childhood.

Utilitarianism   An approach to social policy which would, in theory at least, secure 'the greatest good for the greatest number'.

Welfarism (in juvenile justice)   A concept that children who commit criminal offences are not merely criminals, but have unmet social needs. The issue for the state should not therefore be one of 'punishment' but of 'treatment'. Using metaphors of sickness in this way, it is assumed that social work or psychiatric intervention in the 'sick' family can address the offending behaviour. As with 'pathology' and 'medicalization' the effect can be to deny the offender citizenship rights, so that effectively more painful and intrusive measures (such as removal into care) could be justified on the grounds that even a minor offence could be seen as a symptom of unmet 'need'.

Zero tolerance   A concept first imported to the UK from the US. In the early 1990s it had a specific application in relation to campaigns against violence against women: the 'Z' campaign which began in Edinburgh and was subsequently adopted by UK local authorities. The aim of this campaign was to use graphic representation (advertising hoardings, the 'Z' logo on local authority minibuses, public service vehicles, etc.) to draw attention to the physical and sexual abuse of women and children and to call for 'zero tolerance' of domestic violence. This original and specific application has since been lost as 'zero tolerance', firstly, became taken up in various ways by police forces to characterize more intensive policing of minor infractions, and, secondly, passed into general parlance and political rhetoric as a social attitude. It has now become a cultural and rhetorical device of popular authoritarianism.

References

Abrams, M. (1959) *The Teenage Consumer*. London: London Press Exchange.

Alcock, P. and Harris, P. (1982) *Welfare Law and Order*. London: Macmillan.

Allen, F.A. (1964) *The Borderland of Criminal Justice: Essays in Law and Criminology*. Chicago: Chicago University Press.

Anderson, S., Kinsey, R., Loader, I. and Smith, G. (1994) *Cautionary Tales: Young People and Policing in Edinburgh*. Aldershot: Avebury.

Aries, P. (1973) *Centuries of Childhood*. Harmondsworth: Penguin.

Audit Commission (1996) *Misspent Youth: Young People and Crime*. Abingdon: Audit Commission Publications.

Bailey, V. (1987) *Delinquency and Citizenship: Reclaiming the Young Offender 1914–1948*. Oxford: Clarendon Press.

Baldwin, J. and Bottoms, A. (1976) *The Urban Criminal*. London: Tavistock.

Barker, M. (1997) The Newson Report: a case study in common sense, in M. Barker and J. Petley (eds) *Ill Effects: The Media/Violence Debate*. London: Routledge.

Barker, M. and Petley, J. (eds) (1997) *Ill Effects: The Media/Violence Debate*. London: Routledge.

Bean, P. (1976) *Rehabilitation and Deviance*. London: Routledge and Kegan Paul.

Beynon, J. and Solomos, J. (eds) (1987) *The Roots of Urban Unrest*. Oxford: Pergamon.

Bottomley, A.K. and Pease, K. (1986) *Crime and Punishment: Interpreting the Data*. Milton Keynes: Open University Press.

Bottoms, A.E. (1974) On the decriminalisation of the English Juvenile Courts, in R. Hood (ed.) *Crime, Criminology and Public Policy*. London: Heinemann.

Bottoms, A.E. and Pratt, J. (1989) Intermediate treatment for girls in England and Wales, in M. Cain (ed.) *Growing up Good: Policing the Behaviour of Girls in Europe*. London: Sage.

Bottoms, A.E. and Stevenson, S. (1992) What went wrong? Criminal justice policy in England and Wales, 1945–1970, in D. Downes (ed.) *Unravelling Criminal Justice*. Basingstoke: Macmillan.

Bowlby, J. (1951) *Maternal Care and Mental Health*. London: HMSO.

Box, S. (1983) *Power, Crime and Mystification*. London: Tavistock.

Braithwaite, J. (1989) *Crime, Shame and Reintegration*. Cambridge: CUP.

Brake, M. and Hale, C. (1992) *Public Order and Private Lives*. London: Routledge.

British Journal of Criminology (1988) Special edition, 28(2).

Brody, S.R. (1976) *The Effectiveness of Sentencing*, Home Office Research Study No. 35. London: HMSO.

Brown, S. (1992) 'Doing time: crime and everyday life on Blue Hall'. Unpublished report to Banks of the Wear Housing Association. Middlesbrough: Research Action.

Brown, S. (1994a) 'Whose challenge? Youth, crime and everyday life in Middlesbrough'. Published report to Middlesbrough City Challenge Partnership. Middlesbrough: City Challenge Partnership.

Brown, S. (1994b) 'Time of change? Adult views of youth and crime in Middlesbrough'. Published report to Middlesbrough City Challenge Partnership. Middlesbrough: Middlesbrough City Challenge.

Brown, S. (1995) Crime and safety in whose 'community'? *Youth and Policy*, 48: 27–48.

Burt, C. (1925) *The Young Delinquent*. London: University of London Press.

Cain, M. (ed.) (1989) *Growing up Good: Policing the Behaviour of Girls in Europe*. London: Sage.

Campbell, A. (1984) *The Girls in the Gang*. Oxford: Blackwell.

Campbell, B. (1988) *Unofficial Secrets: Child Sexual Abuse: The Cleveland Case*. London: Virago Press.

Campbell, B. (1993) *Goliath: Britain's Dangerous Places*. London: Methuen.

Carlen, P. (1988) *Women, Crime and Poverty*. Milton Keynes: Open University Press.

Carlen, P. (1996) *Jigsaw – A Political Criminology of Youth Homelessness*. Buckingham: Open University Press.

Carlen, P., Hicks, J., O'Dwyer, J., Christina, D. and Tchaikovsky, C. (1985) *Criminal Women*. Cambridge: Polity Press.

Carter, M. (1966) *Into Work*. Harmondsworth: Penguin.

Cavadino, M. and Dignan, J. (1997) *The Penal System* (2nd edn). London: Sage.

Chesney-Lind, M. (1989) Girl's crime and woman's place: toward a feminist model of female delinquency, *Crime and Delinquency*, 35(1): 5–29.

Chibnall, S. (1977) *Law and Order News*. London: Tavistock.

Christie, N. (1985) Punishment, in A. Kuper and J. Kuper (eds) *The Social Science Encyclopaedia*. London: Routledge and Kegan Paul.

Clarke, J. (1976) The skinheads and the magical recovery of community, in S. Hall and T. Jefferson (eds) *Resistance through Rituals*. London: Macmillan.

Clarke, J. (1980) Social democratic delinquents and Fabian families, in National Deviancy Conference (eds) *Permissiveness and Control*. London: Macmillan.

Clarke, J. (1985) Whose justice? The politics of juvenile control, *International Journal of the Sociology of Law*, 13: 407–21.

Cloward, R. and Ohlin, L. (1960) *Delinquency and Opportunity*. London: Collier Macmillan.

Cockburn, T. (1995) *The Devil in the City: Working Class Children in Manchester 1860–1914*. Paper presented to the British Sociological Association, University of Leicester, April.

Cohen, A.K. (1955) *Delinquent Boys*. London: Free Press.

Cohen, P. (1997) *Rethinking the Youth Question: Education, Labour and Cultural Studies*. London: Macmillan.

Cohen, S. (1973) *Folk Devils and Moral Panics: The Creation of the Mods and Rockers*. St Alban's: Paladin.

Cohen, S. (1985) *Visions of Social Control*. Cambridge: Polity Press.

Cohen, S. (1988) *Against Criminology*. New Brunswick, NJ: Transaction Books.

Coleman, C. and Moynihan, J. (1996) *Understanding Crime Data*. Buckingham: Open University Press.

Connell, R.W. (1987) *Gender and Power: Society, the Person and Sexual Politics*. Cambridge: Polity Press.

Corby, B. (1997) The mistreatment of young people, in J. Roche and S. Tucker (eds) *Youth in Society*. London: Sage.

Corrigan, P. (1976) Doing nothing, in S. Hall and T. Jefferson (eds) *Resistance through Rituals*. London: Hutchinson.

Creighton, S.J. and Noyes, P. (1989) *Child Abuse Trends in England and Wales 1983–1987*. London: National Society for the Prevention of Cruelty to Children.

Davies, B. (1986) *Threatening Youth: Towards a National Youth Policy*. Milton Keynes: Open University Press.

Davis, J. (1990) *Youth and the Condition of Britain: Images of Adolescent Conflict*. London: Athlone Press.

de Haan, W. (1990) *The Politics of Redress: Crime, Punishment and Penal Abolition*. London: Unwin Hyman.

Ditchfield, J. (1976) *Police Cautioning in England and Wales*, Home Office Research Study No. 37. London: HMSO.

Donzelot, J. (1980) *The Policing of Families*. London: Hutchinson.

Douglas, M. (1994) *Purity and Danger: An Analysis of the Concepts of Pollution and Taboo*. London: Routledge.

Downes, D. (1966) *The Delinquent Solution*. London: Routledge and Kegan Paul.

Downes, D. (1988) The sociology of crime and social control in Britain, 1960–1987, *British Journal of Criminology*, 28(2): 45–55.

Downes, D. and Rock, P. (1988) *Understanding Deviance: A Guide to the Sociology of Crime and Rule Breaking* (2nd edn). Oxford: Clarendon Press.

Duff, R.A. and Garland, D. (eds) (1994) *A Reader on Punishment*. Oxford: Oxford University Press.

Ennew, J. (1986) *The Sexual Exploitation of Children*. Cambridge: Polity Press.

Farrington, D.P. (1994) Human development and criminal careers, in M. Maguire, R. Morgan and R. Reiner (eds) *The Oxford Handbook of Criminology*. Oxford: Clarendon Press.

Förnas, J. and Bolin, G. (eds) (1995) *Youth Cultures in Late Modernity*. London: Sage.

Foucault, M. (1990) *The History of Sexuality: Volume I*. Harmondsworth: Penguin.

Furnham, A. and Gunter, B. (1989) *The Anatomy of Adolescence: Young People's Social Attitudes in Britain*. London: Routledge.

Fyvel, T. (1963) *The Insecure Offenders*. Harmondsworth: Penguin.

Garland, D. (1994) Of crimes and criminals: the development of criminology in Britain, in M. Maguire, R. Morgan and R. Reiner (eds) *The Oxford Handbook of Criminology*. Oxford: Clarendon Press.

Garratt, D. (1997) Youth cultures and subcultures, in J. Roche and S. Tucker (eds) *Youth in Society*. London: Sage.

Gaskell, E. (1981) *Mary Barton: A Tale of Manchester Life*. Harmondsworth: Penguin.

Gelsthorpe, L. and Morris, A. (1994) Juvenile justice 1945–1992, in M. Maguire, R. Morgan and R. Reiner (eds) *The Oxford Handbook of Criminology*. Oxford: Clarendon Press.

Gibbons, S. (1996) Reclaiming the streets, in *Police Review*, 13 September: 18–22.

Gibson, B. (1995) Young people, bad news, enduring principles, *Youth and Policy*, 48: 64–70.

Gibson, B. *et al.* (1994) *The Youth Court – One Year Onwards*. Winchester: Waterside Press.

Giddens, A. (1991) *Modernity and Self Identity: Self and Society in the Late Modern Age*. Cambridge: Polity.

Gill, O. (1977) *Luke Street: Housing Policy, Conflict and the Creation of the Delinquent Area*. London: Macmillan.

Goodey, J. (1994) Fear of crime: what can children tell us? *International Review of Victimology*, 3: 125–210.

Goodey, J. (1995) *Boys Don't Cry: Masculinities, Fear of Crime, and Fearlessness*. Paper presented to the American Society of Criminology Conference, Boston MA, November.

Gramsci, A. (1978) *Selections from the Prison Notebooks*. London: Lawrence and Wishart.

Griffin, C. (1993) *Representations of Youth: The Study of Youth in Britain and America*. Cambridge: Polity.

Guardian/ICM (1996) Dream teens, *The Guardian* 14 May.

Hagan, J. (1989) *Structural Criminology*. New Brunswick, NJ: Rutgers University Press.

Hagan, J., Simpson, J.H. and Gillis, A.R. (1979) The sexual stratification of social control: a gender-based perspective on crime and delinquency, *British Journal of Sociology*, 30: 25–38.

Hagell, A. and Newburn, T. (1994) *Persistent Young Offenders*. London: Policy Studies Institute.

Hall, G.S. (1904) *Adolescence: Its Psychology and Its Relation to Physiology, Anthropology, Sociology, Sex, Crime, Religion and Education*: 2 vols. New York: D. Appleton.

Hall, S. and Jefferson, T. (eds) (1976) *Resistance through Rituals: Youth Subcultures in Post-War Britain*. London: Hutchinson.

Hall, S., Critcher, C., Jefferson, T., Clarke, J. and Roberts, B. (1978) *Policing the Crisis: Mugging, the State, and Law and Order*. London: Macmillan.

Harris, J. (1993) *Private Lives, Public Spirit: Britain 1870–1914*. Harmondsworth: Penguin.

Harris, R.J. (1985) Towards just welfare, *British Journal of Criminology*, 25(1): 31–45.

Harris, R. and Webb, D. (1987) *Welfare, Power and Juvenile Justice*. London: Tavistock.

Hartless, J., Ditton, J., Nair, G. and Phillips, S. (1995) More sinned against than sinning: a study of young teenagers' experiences of crime, *British Journal of Criminology*, 35(1): 114–33.

Harwin, J. (1982) The battle for the delinquent, in *The Yearbook of Social Policy in Britain 1980–1981*. London: Routledge and Kegan Paul.

Heidensohn, F.M. (1968) The deviance of women: a critique and an enquiry, *British Journal of Sociology*, 19(2): 160–75.

Heidensohn, F. (1994) Gender and crime, in M. Maguire, R. Morgan and R. Reiner (eds) *The Oxford Handbook of Criminology*. Oxford: Clarendon Press.

Heidensohn, F. (1996) *Women and Crime* (2nd edn). London: Macmillan.

Hendrick, H. (1990) Constructions and reconstructions of British childhood: an interpretive survey 1800 to the present, in A. James and A. Prout (eds) *Constructing and Reconstructing Childhood*. London: Falmer.

Hirschi, T. (1969) *Causes of Delinquency*. Berkeley: University of California Press.

Hockey, J. and James, A. (1993) *Growing up and Growing Old: Ageing and Dependency in the Life Course*. London: Sage.

Holland, P. (1997) Living for libido; or Child's Play IV; the imagery of childhood and call for censorship, in M. Barker and J. Petley (eds) *Ill Effects: The Media/Violence Debate*. London: Routledge.

Home Office (1927) *Report of the Departmental Committee on the Treatment of Young Offenders*, Cmd 2831 [The Molony Report]. London: HMSO.

Home Office (1946) *The Care of Children Committee*, Cmd 6922 [The Curtis Report]. London: HMSO.

Home Office (1960) *Report on the Committee on Children and Young Persons*, Cmnd 1191 [The Ingleby Report]. London: HMSO.

Home Office (1965) *The Child, The Family and the Young Offender*, Cmnd 2742. London: HMSO.

Home Office (1968) *Children in Trouble*, Cmnd 3601. London: HMSO.

Home Office (1976) *The Children and Young Persons Act, 1969: Observations on the Eleventh Report of the Expenditure Committee*, Cmnd 6494. London: HMSO.

Home Office (1980) *Young Offenders*, Cmnd 8045. London: HMSO.

Home Office (1984) *Tougher Regimes in Detention Centres: Report of an Evaluation by the Young Offender Psychology Unit*. London: HMSO.

Home Office (1990) *Crime, Justice and Protecting the Public*, Cm 965. London: HMSO.

Home Office (1995) *National Standards for the Supervision of Offenders in the Community*. London: Home Office.

Home Office (1995) *Young People, Victimization and the Police: British Crime Survey Findings on Experiences and Attitudes of 12–15 Year Olds*, Home Office Research Study No. 140. London: HMSO.

Home Office (1996) *Protecting the Public*, Cm 3190. London: HMSO.

Hood, R. (1974) Criminology and penal change: a case study of the nature and impact of some recent advice to governments, in R. Hood (ed.) *Crime, Criminology and Public Policy*. London: Heinemann.

Hornby, N. (1992) *Fever Pitch*. London: Gollancz.

House of Commons Expenditure Committee (1975) *Eleventh Report from the Expenditure Committee: The Children and Young Persons Act, 1969*. London: HMSO.

Hudson, A. (1989) Troublesome girls, in M. Cain (ed.) *Growing up Good: Policing the Behaviour of Girls in Europe*. London: Sage.

Hudson, B.A. (1996) *Understanding Justice: An Introduction to Ideas, Perspectives, and Controversies in Modern Penal Theory*. Buckingham: Open University Press.

Inglis, F. (1993) *Cultural Studies*. Oxford: Blackwell.

James, A. and Prout, A. (eds) (1990) *Constructing and Reconstructing Childhood*. London: Falmer.

Jefferson, T. (1976) Cultural responses of the teds: the defence of space and status, in S. Hall and T. Jefferson (eds) *Resistance through Rituals*. London: Hutchinson.

Jefferson, T. (1994) Theorising masculine subjectivity, in T. Newburn and E.A. Stanko (eds) *Just Boys Doing Business: Men, Masculinities and Crime*. London: Routledge.

Jenks, C. (1996) *Childhood*. London: Routledge.

Johnston, L. (1997) New Labour and the usual suspects, *Chartist*, March–April: 14–15.

Jones, T., Maclean, B. and Young, J. (eds) (1986) *The Islington Crime Survey*. Aldershot: Gower.

Kelly, L. and Radford, J. (1987) The problem of men: feminist perspectives on sexual violence, in P. Scraton (ed.) *Law, Order and the Authoritarian State*. Milton Keynes: Open University Press.

Kidd-Hewitt, D. and Osborne, R. (eds) (1995) *Crime and the Media: The Postmodern Spectacle*. London: Pluto Press.

King, M. (1991) The political construction of crime prevention: a contrast between the French and British experience, in K. Stenson and D. Cowell (eds) *The Politics of Crime Control*. London: Sage.

Kinsey, R. (1985) *First Report of the Merseyside Crime Survey*. Liverpool: Merseyside County Council.

Latour, B. (1986) The powers of association, in J. Law (ed.) *Power, Action and Belief: Towards a New Sociology of Knowledge?* London: Routledge and Kegan Paul.

Lees, S. (1989) Learning to love: sexual reputation, morality and the social control of girls, in M. Cain (ed.) *Growing up Good: Policing the Behaviour of Girls in Europe*. London: Sage.

Leonard, E.B. (1982) *Women, Crime, and Society: A Critique of Theoretical Criminology*. New York: Longman.

Levi, M. (1994) Masculinities and white-collar crime, in T. Newburn and E.A. Stanko (eds) *Just Boys Doing Business: Men, Masculinities and Crime*. London: Routledge.

Lipton, D., Martinson, R. and Wilks, J. (1975) *The Effectiveness of Correctional Treatment: A Survey of Evaluation Studies*. New York: Praeger.

Lombroso, C. and Ferrero, W. (1895) *The Female Offender*. London: T. Fisher Unwin.

Lury, C. (1996) *Consumer Culture*. Cambridge: Polity Press.

Maguire, M., Morgan, R. and Reiner, R. (eds) (1997) *The Oxford Handbook of Criminology*. Oxford: Clarendon Press.

Matthews, R. and Young, J. (eds) (1992) *Issues in Realist Criminology*. London: Sage.

Matza, D. (1964) *Delinquency and Drift*. New York: Wiley.

Matza, D. (1969) *Becoming Deviant*. Englewood Cliffs, NJ: Prentice Hall.

Matza, D. and Sykes, G. (1961) Juvenile delinquency and subterranean values, *American Sociological Review*, 26: 712–19.

Mawby, R.I. (1979) The victimization of juveniles: a comparative study of publicly owned housing in Sheffield, *Journal of Crime and Delinquency*, 16: 98–114.

McInerney, J. (1993) *Bright Lights, Big City*. London: Penguin.

McLaughlin, E. and Muncie, J. (1993) Juvenile delinquency, in R. Dallos and E. McLaughlin (eds) *Social Problems and the Family*. London: Sage.

McRobbie, A. (1991) *Feminism and Youth Culture: From Jackie to Just Seventeen*. London: Macmillan.

McRobbie, A. and Nava, M. (eds) (1984) *Gender and Generation*. London: Macmillan.

Merton, R.K. (1993) Social structure and anomie, in C. Lemert (ed.) *Social Theory: The Multicultural Readings*. Boulder, CO: Westview Press.

Messerschmidt, J.W. (1993) *Masculinities and Crime: Critique and Reconceptualization of Theory*. Lanham, MY: Rowman and Littlefield.

Messerschmidt, J.W. (1994) Schooling, masculinities and youth crime by white boys, in T. Newburn and E.A. Stanko (eds) *Just Boys Doing Business? Men, Masculinities and Crime*. London: Routledge.

Miller, W.B. (1958) Lower class culture as a generating milieu of gang delinquency, *Journal of Social Issues*, 14(3): 5–19.

Millham, S., Bullock, R. and Hosie, K. (1978) *Locking up Children*. Farnborough: Saxon House.

Ministry of Education (1959) *15–18* [The Crowther Report]. London: HMSO.

Morgan, J. and Zedner, L. (1992) *Child Victims: Crime, Impact and Criminal Justice*. Oxford: Clarendon Press.

Morgan, P. (1981) The Children's Act: sacrificing justice to social worker's needs? in C. Brewer *et al.* (eds) *Criminal Welfare on Trial*. London: Social Affairs Unit.

Morris, A. (1987) *Women, Crime and Criminal Justice*. Oxford: Basil Blackwell.

Morris, A. and Giller, H. (1987) *Understanding Juvenile Justice*. London: Croom Helm.

Morris, A. and McIsaac, M. (1978) *Juvenile Justice?* London: Heinemann.

Morris, A., Giller, H., Szwed, E. and Geach, H. (1980) *Justice for Children*. London: Macmillan.

Morse, M. (1965) *The Unattached*. Harmondsworth: Penguin.

Muncie, J. (1984) *The Trouble with Kids Today*. London: Hutchinson.

Muncie, J. (1987) Much ado about nothing? The sociology of moral panics, *Social Studies Review*, 3(2): 42–7.

Muncie, J. and McLaughlin, E. (eds) (1996) *The Problem of Crime*. London: Sage.

Murdock, G. (1997) Reservoirs of dogma: an archaeology of popular anxieties, in M. Barker and J. Petley (eds) *Ill Effects*. London: Routledge.

Newburn, T. (1995) *Crime and Criminal Justice Policy*. London: Longman.

Parker, H. (1974) *View from the Boys*. Newton Abbot: David and Charles.

Parsloe, P. (1978) *Juvenile Justice in Britain and the United States*. London: Routledge and Kegan Paul.

Pearson, G. (1983) *Hooligan: A History of Respectable Fears*. London: Macmillan.

Pearson, G. (1994) *Youth, Crime and Society*, in M. Maguire, R. Morgan and R. Reiner (eds) *The Oxford Handbook of Criminology*. Oxford: Clarendon Press.

abc.

Pearson, G. (1995) Lawlessness, modernity and social change: a historical appraisal, *Theory, Culture and Society*, 2(3): 15–36.

Penal Affairs Consortium (1995) *Boot Camps for Young Offenders*. London: Penal Affairs Consortium.

Phillips, D. (1977) *Crime and Authority in Victorian England*. London: Croom Helm.

Pilcher, J. (1995) *Age and Generation in Modern Britain*. Oxford: Oxford University Press.

Pinchbeck, I. and Hewitt, M. (1973) *Children in English Society: Vol. II*. London: Routledge and Kegan Paul.

Pitts, J. (1988) *The Politics of Juvenile Crime*. London: Sage.

Pitts, J. (1995) Scare in the community: Britain in a moral panic, *Community Care*, 4–10 May.

Pollak, O. (1950) *The Criminality of Women*. Philadelphia: University of Pennsylvania Press.

Pratt, J. (1983) Intermediate treatment and the normalisation crisis, *Howard Journal*, 22: 19–37.

Pratt, J. (1990) Crime, time, youth and punishment, *Contemporary Crises*, 14(3): 220–42.

Radzinowicz, L. and Hood, R. (1986) *A History of English Criminal Law. Vol. V: The Emergence of Penal Policy*. London: Stephens and Sons.

Redhead, S. (1990) The end-of-the-century-party: youth and pop towards 2000. Manchester: Manchester University Press.

Redhead, S. (1995) *Unpopular Cultures: The Birth of Law and Popular Culture*. Manchester: Manchester University Press.

Roche, J. (1997) Children's rights: participation and dialogue, in J. Roche and S. Tucker (eds) *Youth in Society*. London: Sage.

Rose, D. (1995) Back to jackboot justice, *Observer* 12 March.

Rutherford, A. (1996) *Transforming Criminal Justice Policy*. Winchester: Waterside Press.

Rutter, M. and Giller, H. (1983) *Juvenile Delinquency*. Harmondsworth: Penguin.

Save the Children (no date) *Children's Rights in the U.K.* Information pamphlet. London: Save the Children.

Sibley, D. (1995) *Geographies of Exclusion*. London: Routledge.

Smart, C. (1976) *Women, Crime and Criminology: A Feminist Critique*. London: Routledge and Kegan Paul.

Smith, D.J. (1994) *The Sleep of Reason: The James Bulger Case*. London: Century.

Storch, R.D. (1980) The plague of the blue locusts: police reform and popular resistance in Northern England 1840–1857, in M. Fitzgerald, G. McLennon and J. Pawson (eds) *Crime and Society*. London: Routledge.

Taylor, I. and Taylor, L. (eds) (1973) *Politics and Deviance: Papers from the National Deviancy Conference*. Harmondsworth: Penguin.

Taylor, I., Walton, P. and Young, J. (1973) *The New Criminology: For a Social Theory of Deviance*. London: Routledge and Kegan Paul.

Taylor, L., Lacey, R. and Bracken, D. (1979) *In Whose Best Interests? The Unjust Treatment of Children in Courts and Institutions*. Nottingham: Cobden Trust/MIND.

Thorpe, D.H., Smith, D.B., Green, C.J. and Paley, J.H. (1980) *Out of Care*. London: Allen and Unwin.

Tierney, J. (1996) *Criminology: Theory and Context*. London: Prentice Hall/Harvester Wheatsheaf.

Walklate, S. (1989) *Victimology: The Victim and the Criminal Justice Process*. London: Unwin Hyman.

Welsh, I. (1993) *Trainspotting*. London: Secker and Warburg.

Williams, J. and Taylor, R. (1994) Boys keep swinging: masculinity and football culture in England, in T. Newburn and E.A. Stanko (eds) *Just Boys Doing Business? Men, Masculinities and Crime*. London: Routledge.

Willis, P. (1977) *Learning to Labour: How Working Class Kids Get Working Class Jobs*. Farnborough: Saxon House.

Willis, P. (1990) *Common Culture*. Buckingham: Open University Press.

Wilmott, P. (1966) *Adolescent Boys of East London*. London: Routledge and Kegan Paul.

Windlesham, Lord (1993) *Penal Policy in the Making: Volume 2 – Responses to Crime*. Oxford: Clarendon Press.

Wullschlager, J. (1995) *Inventing Wonderland*. London: Methuen.

Young, A. (1996) *Imagining Crime*. London: Sage.

Young, J. (1974) Mass media, drugs and deviance, in P. Rock and M. McKintosh (eds) *Deviance and Social Control*. London: Tavistock.

Young, J. (1988) Radical criminology in Britain: the emergence of a competing paradigm, *British Journal of Criminology*, 28(2): 159–83.

Young, J. (1992) Ten points of realism, in J. Young and R. Matthews (eds) *Rethinking Criminology: The Realist Debate*. London: Sage.

Young, J. (1994) Incessant chatter: recent paradigms in criminology, in M. Maguire, R. Morgan and R. Reiner (eds) *The Oxford Handbook of Criminology*. Oxford: Clarendon Press.

Young, J. (1997) Left realist criminology: radical in its analysis, realist in its policy, in M. Maguire, R. Morgan and R. Reiner (eds) *The Oxford Handbook of Criminology*. Oxford: Clarendon Press.

Young, J. and Matthews, R. (eds) (1992) *Rethinking Criminology: The Realist Debate*. London: Sage.

Zedner, L. (1994) Victims, in M. Maguire, R. Morgan and R. Reiner (eds) *The Oxford Handbook of Criminology*. Oxford: Clarendon Press.

Index

Abrams, M., 25–6
abuse, 87, 96
  physical, 60, 82, 84–7
  sexual, 60, 82, 84–7, 88–90
academic approach, 2, 18
  see also criminology
academic research, and practical
    policies, 22, 76
academics, male, 30, 98
Acts of Parliament
  Children Act (1908), 55, 61
  Children Act (1948), 57
  Children Act (1989), 70, 83, 87
  Children and Young Persons Act
    (1933), 56, 61
  Children and Young Persons Act
    (1963), 58, 61
  Children and Young Persons Act
    (1969), 43, 54–5, 59–60, 61,
    62–3, 76, 87
  Crime (Sentences) Act (1997), 75
  Criminal Justice Act (1948), 57
  Criminal Justice Act (1982), 65–6
  Criminal Justice Act (1988), 66
  Criminal Justice Act (1991), 54, 65,
    70, 71, 72, 75
  Criminal Justice Act (1993), 71
  Criminal Justice and Public Order Act
    (1994), 72–3
  Education Act (1870), 14
  Education Act (1944), 25
  Factory Act (1833), 9
  Juvenile Offenders Act (1847), 55

  Police and Criminal Evidence Act
    (1984), 67
  Public Order Act (1985), 67
adolescence, 2, 11, 12, 98
  definitions of, 14–15
  and delinquency, 10
adults
  and crime, 3, 93, 95, 117
  harassment of young people by, 91
  middle class, concepts of childhood,
    6–8
  as victims, 93–5
Advisory Council on the Penal System, 65
aetiology, see crime, causes of
affluence, 25–6, 40, 45, 61
age
  concepts of, 1–2, 4
  of criminal responsibility, 58, 59, 61,
    83
  and criminalization, 16
  and power, 5
alcohol, 74, 75
Anderson, S., 91–2, 93
anomie, 23, 28
anthropology, 22
anxiety
  adult, 11, 34, 84, 116
  and control, 16
  about crime, 99
  and popular culture, 46–7
  youth as focus of, 33, 43, 44, 46–7,
    49, 51
  see also fears

Appeal Court, 81
area studies, 29
assault, 4, 82, 87, 91
attendance centres, 57, 61, 62, 63, 64
authoritarianism, 44, 51, 79, 116

bail, 73
Baker, Kenneth, 71
begging, 56
behaviour modification, 63
Bills
    Crime and Disorder Bill (proposed,
        1997), 75, 81
    Criminal Justice and Public Order Bill
        (1993), 80–1
Birmingham School, 31, 33
black male youth, 43
black youth, 44
Blair, Tony, 71
boot camps, 3, 73, 84
borstals, 61
boys, see offenders, young male
British Crime Survey, 75, 91–2, 94
British Journal of Delinquency, 21
Bulger case, 2–3, 49–51, 62, 80, 81
burglaries, 95
Burt, Cyril, 20–1, 26–7
Butler Sloss Inquiry, 85

Callaghan, James, 60
Campbell, Bea, 49
capitalism, 23, 31, 34, 44, 115
    deregulated, 110
    industrial, 7, 13
care, 54, 55, 63, 116
    and control, 60
    non-residential, 63
    parental, 58
care institutions, and victimization,
        87–90
care orders, 62
Carroll, Lewis, 6–7
cars, and crime, 47–9, 70–1, 94, 111
casework theory, 57
cautions, formal, 65, 66, 67, 72, 74
    reduced use of, 81
    and warnings, 61, 75, 77
censorship, 51

Centre for Contemporary Cultural
        Studies, 29–30, 31, 32, 34, 42,
        106
change
    economic, 25–6
    social, 7, 11, 24–6, 33
Chibnall, S., 42
Chicago School, 21–3, 28
child labour, 8–10, 12
childhood
    concepts of, 1, 2–3, 51, 114
        Victorian, 5–12
    modern, 12
    as 'other', 12, 20
    regulation of, 10–11
    as social category, 11, 37
    wartime, 24
    see also children; young people; youth
children
    dispossession of, 12
    real lives of, 11–12
    rights of, 83
    victimization of, 84–90
    welfare needs of, 59
    young, and crime, 46, 49–51
citizenship, 68, 79, 82, 84, 118, 119
    lack of, 95
civil servants, 59
Clarke, Kenneth, 71
class
    and crime, 30
    and culture, 33
    see also middle classes; working class
class relations, 30, 34
Clerks to the Justices, 59, 62, 71
Cohen, Phil, 31–2, 42–3
Cohen, Stanley, 40–1, 42, 43, 45
community, 32
    reintegration of offenders into, 74
    working class, 34
community punishment, 69, 70, 73
community service orders, 65
community-based sentencing, 68–9
conflict, generational, 32
conformity, 100–2, 103, 104
control, 54, 55, 63, 110, 116
    adult ideas of, 3
    and anxiety, 16

and care, 60
and conformity, 100–2
costs of, 67
education as, 25
families as institutions of, 96
parental, 70
and punishment, 64, 82
social, 21, 55, 56, 75, 87
and welfare, 61–2
and social workers, 65
and women, 101
of young people, 54, 56, 60, 77, 82
cost effectiveness, 74
courts, 41, 55
and female offenders, 103
and media representations, 41
see also Juvenile Courts; Magistrates'
Courts
crime
abuse as, 88
and adults, 3, 29, 93, 95, 117
and affluence, 25
and cars, 47–9, 70–1, 94, 111
causes of, 50–1, 93, 96, 105
and class, 30
effects of, 94–5, 96
and gender, 110, 112, 117
juvenile, 58, 60, 71, 72
and male youth, 98
organized, 22
and patriarchy, 30
recorded, 62
reported to police, 91–2
statistics, 91
study of, see criminology
and women, 100, 102
young people's fear of, 95, 111
and youth, 1, 11, 88, 107, 110–11,
114, 117, 118, 119
construction of, 54, 79, 95, 96,
113, 115
Crime and Disorder Bill (proposed,
1997), 75, 81
Criminal Injuries Compensation Board,
89
criminal justice policy, 68–9, 116
Criminal Justice and Public Order Bill
(1993), 80–1

criminal justice system, 19, 61, 66, 69,
85, 87, 96
and females, 102–3, 106
criminalization, 34
and age, 16
of non-school attendance, 66
of youth, 29, 31, 82, 115
criminals, see offenders
criminology, 76, 85, 90, 103–6, 112,
116
academic approach to, 19
constructing youth, 18
crisis in, 93
cultural, 31
feminist, 31, 103–6, 107
and male youth, 98
and masculinities, 106–7
and popular representation, 115
postwar, 23–9
and women, 99–100, 103–6
and youth, 18–21, 23, 28, 35, 96,
102, 114–15
see also Schools of criminology
cruelty, to children, 90
culture
and class, 33
dominant, 33
local, 29
parent, 33
popular, 12, 39, 45, 118
and anxiety, 46
regulation of, 13–14
subordinate, 33
working class, 33
youth and, 32
see also pop culture
curfews, 75, 81
custodial sentencing, 62, 66, 67, 69,
71
see also incarceration; prison
custody
effectiveness of, 67
of juveniles, 61, 65, 66

decriminalization, 43, 59
delinquency
and adolescence, 10
as category, 29

climate of, 25
and criminology, 18, 23, 29
and deprivation, 57, 59, 87
and families, 71
gender differences in, 101
juvenile, concepts of, 12, 64
and masculinity, 109–10
and neglect, 56, 57
and normal growing up, 59, 60
and research, 20–1, 22–4
study of, 15
see also crime; offenders
demonization, 41
of youth, 31, 46, 75, 79, 116
depopulation, 31
deprivation
    and delinquency, 57, 59, 87
    social, 28–9
deregulation, financial, 45
detention, long-term, 73
detention centres, 57, 61, 63, 65, 66
deviance
    British sociology of, 30
    concepts of, 1, 24
    and cultural expectations, 4
deviancy amplification spiral, 40
deviant adaptation, 23
disabilities, 94
discipline, 40, 58, 64, 73, 88, 117
    parental, 70, 96–7
    social, 67, 92
    and social workers, 65
    and welfare policies, 68
discourse
    academic, 115
    popular, 18, 116
discourses
    of childhood, 5
    of difference, 16–17
    of fear, 46
    of moral panic, 51
    of youth, 13, 16–17
disenfranchisement, 45
disorder, urban, 45, 47
disturbance, emotional, 57
drugs, 74, 106

economies, local, 29

economy, British, 12, 13, 44
education, 10, 21, 56, 63, 77
    and children's rights, 83
    as control, 25
    and dependency, 12
    elementary, 14
    higher, 30
    irrelevance of, 110
    and middle class, 13
    and opportunity, 44
    policies on, 68
    universal secondary, 25
    young people's attitudes to, 92
elderly, see old age
electronic monitoring, 74, 75
emotional disturbance, 57
employment, 44, 74, 77, 100
    policies on, 68
environment, young people's attitudes
    to, 92
environmental crimes, 95
ethnic groups, 22
ethnic minorities, 94
ethnography, 29, 34, 35
European Court of Human Rights,
    81
exclusion
    cultural, 35
    of social groups, 15–16
expectations
    cultural, and deviance, 4
    social, 1

families
    as control institutions, 96
    and delinquency, 71
    and gender roles, 100
    and Juvenile Courts, 56
    separation from, 60
    victimization in, 84–7
    welfare needs of, 59
    working class, 32, 77
        morality of, 58
    young people's attitudes to, 92
    and youth crime, 70, 74
Family Councils, 59
family failure, 58, 77
family justice, 55

fear, of crime
  boys', 111
  young people's, 95
fears, 37, 47, 92, 95
  middle class, 9–10, 11, 14
  see also anxiety
femininity, 99, 109
feminism, 86, 103, 108
feminist criminology, 31, 103–6, 107
folk devils, 41, 43, 44, 47, 71
football violence, 67
Frankfurt School, 39
fraud, 95, 105, 110

gangs, 13, 22, 23, 106, 109
  mods and rockers, 40–1
Gaskell, Elizabeth, 9
gender
  and crime, 101, 110, 112, 117
  and youth crime, 107
gender relations, 105
gender roles, 100, 107
genetic theory, 27
girls, 13, 33, 68
  adolescent, 15
  and criminology, 99, 105–6
  and gender roles, 100–1
  invisibility of, 20
  sexuality of, 103, 106
  see also offenders, female; women
governments, 76
  Conservative, 58, 61, 64–5, 67, 76
  Labour, 59, 61, 62–3, 65, 76
  New Labour, 75–7, 81

Hall, S., 32–3, 42–4
harassment, 95
  of young people, 91
health, 77
health service, 85
hegemony, 33
  resistance to, 34
  see also masculinities
Home Office Children's Department, 62
Home Office Criminal Statistics, 75
Home Secretaries
  Baker, Kenneth, 71
  Callaghan, James, 60

Clarke, Kenneth, 71
  Howard, Michael, 50, 71–3, 75,
    80–1
  Hurd, Douglas, 68–9
  Jenkins, Roy, 59
  Straw, Jack, 75–6
  Waddington, David, 70
homelessness, 10, 82, 83
hooliganism, 14
horror movies, 2–3, 50–1
  see also videos
housing, 60, 68, 74, 77, 94
  inner city, 31–2
  policies, 29
Howard, Michael, 50, 71–3, 75, 80–1
Hurd, Douglas, 68–9

ideologies, 25, 33, 80, 102, 118
  capitalist, 31
  of control, 101
  of crime, 44
  of family, 86
  of individual responsibility, 62, 64
  political, 19, 64, 65–6, 67, 69, 75
  ruling, 34
images
  cultural, 115
  of society, 42
  visual
    in news media, 48–9
    sadistic, 51
immigration, 22, 43
incarceration, 21
  see also custodial sentencing; prison
industrial relations, 44
Industrial Schools, 55
industrial unrest, 64
industrialization, 8–9
industries
  high technology, 32
  manufacturing, 45
inequality, 23, 107
  economic, 35
innocence, and childhood, 2, 6–7
inter-textuality, 38–9
intermediate treatment, 63, 68
  intensive, 66
Internet, 38, 51

Jenkins, Roy, 59
Jillings Inquiry, 89
judges, 83
judiciary, 43–4, 69, 76
justice, 53–4
    entitlement to, 82
    and revenge, 72, 73
    youth, and welfare, 53–61
Juvenile Courts, 55–7, 58, 59, 61, 63
    powers of, 64, 65, 71
    to be replaced, 70
juvenile justice policy, 54–5, 77
juvenile justice system, 21, 43, 58, 59,
        74
    changes in, 76–7
    New Labour overhaul of, 75
    unpredictability of, 67

labour
    division of, 33, 101, 102, 107
    organized, 61
Labour movement, 8
Labour party, *see* governments
language, 74
    of law and order rhetoric, 64–5
    and meanings, 53–4, 60
    of punishment, 82
law and order, young people's attitudes
        to, 92
lawyers, 59
legal profession, women in, 102
legislation, 53
leisure, 74
liberalism, 43, 51
liberty
    deprivation of, 54, 60, 64
    restriction of, 69
lifestyle, 26
London, East End, 31–2

magistrates, 59, 61, 62, 63, 72, 76
    and inter-agency management, 66
    and parental control orders, 81
    and sentencing, 67
    use of custody, 66
Magistrates' Association, 62, 71
Magistrates' Courts, 57
Major, John, 80

marginality, 16, 118
marginalization, 114, 116
    of children as victims, 87
    economic, 95
    of males, 98
    of youth, 12, 14, 15, 27–8
Marx, Karl, 7–8
Marxism, 33–4, 44
masculinities, 99, 112, 117
    and criminology, 106–7
    hegemonic, 108, 109–10, 111
    subordinated, 108, 111
masculinity, 23, 106–8
    and delinquency, 109–10
    and youth crime, 107
    see also offenders, young male; youth,
        male
Matza, David, 23–4, 30
meaning, and deviance, 30
meanings
    cultural, 34–5, 39
    and languages, 54
    young people's, 35
media, 18, 79, 80, 85, 90, 92
    and Bulger case, 2–3, 50–1
    and criminology, 115
    and mugging, 42–3
    and news values, 41–2
    popular, 2, 118
        and moral climate, 84
    and society, 38–9
    and victimization, 88–9
    and youth, 40–1, 46–51
    see also tabloids
Merton, R.K., 23
middle age, 1, 2, 3, 114
middle class values, 55
middle classes, 8, 10, 13, 14
    and civilization, 9
    family life of, 9
    fears of, 9–10, 11, 14
    morality of, 7
    and unemployment, 45
miners' strike, 67
minorities
    ethnic, 94
    racial, 44, 45
mistreatment, 87

modernism, 38, 46
modernity, 12, 38, 51, 79
mods and rockers, 40–1, 42, 44
monitoring, electronic, 74, 75
moral backlash, 43–4
moral panic, 34, 48, 62, 71, 72, 115
    and child abuse, 86, 88
    discourse of, 51
    idea of, 39–40, 44–5, 46
    media's need for, 41–2
    and mugging, 43, 44
    post-industrial, 47
morality, 4, 7, 15, 64, 73
    decline of, 39, 43, 45
movies, 39
    horror, 2–3, 50–1
    see also videos
mugging, 42–3, 44, 64
murder, 2, 49–50, 95
music, popular, 40, 46, 51, 81

naming and shaming, 75
National Deviancy Conference, 29–31
National Front, 43
National Standards for the Supervision
        of Offenders, 73
neglect, 55–6, 60
    and delinquency, 56, 57
'New Deviancy', 41
New Labour, see governments
newspapers, see media; tabloids
non-custodial policies, 72
non-custodial sentencing, 66, 67, 69
non-delinquency, 21, 24, 29
normality, 15, 20, 41

offenders
    female, 103–6
    minor/serious, 59, 65, 67
    occasional/persistent, 63, 67
    persistent, 74, 81, 90, 92
    reform of, 56–7, 69
    as victims, 59
    young male, 98–9, 106, 110–11
offending
    petty, and young people, 93, 94–5
    petty/serious, and young people, 92
    those at risk of, 68

old age, 1, 2, 3–4
    infantilization of, 4
    and vulnerability, 94, 114
orders
    care, 62
    community service, 65
    in Crime and Disorder Bill (proposed,
        1997), 75, 81
    parental control, 81
    secure training, 71, 72, 81, 83
    supervision, 62, 65, 66
otherness, 1, 16, 17

paedophilia, 88–9
parental care, 58
parental control orders, 81
parental discipline, 70, 96–7
parenting, inadequate, 77
parents, 56, 59, 64, 71, 73, 74, 117
    rights of, 85, 86, 87
Parliamentary All Party Penal Affairs
        Group, 65, 66
patriarchy, 7, 100, 102
    and crime, 30
permissiveness, 43, 64
police, 12, 14, 61, 64, 76, 83
    attitude to victimization of young
        people, 96
    and car crime, 47–9, 70–1, 111
    crimes reported to, 91–2
    and girls, 103
    and inter-agency management, 66
    and media representations, 41
    and paedophilia, 88
    and persistent offenders, 71
    powers of, 67
    and social work, 66–7, 68
    as state apparatus, 43–4
    surveillance by, 40
    and use of formal cautions, 61
    women in, 102
Police Federation, 62
policing, 21, 84, 94, 96
    of families, 86
    and girls, 102–3
policy, see criminal justice policy;
        juvenile justice policy; youth
        justice

political parties, 55, 76
  Conservative, 59, 61, 64, 69, 71, 75, 80
  see also governments
politicians, 2, 43, 45, 85, 92, 116, 118
pop culture, 26
popular culture, 12, 39, 45, 118
pornography, 88
positivism, 20–1, 24, 29, 30, 100
poverty, 44, 83, 94
Powellism, 43
power, 3, 13, 16, 107, 109
  and age, 5
pre-delinquency, 27
pre-sentence reports, 70, 73
press, *see* media; tabloids
prison, 10, 19, 69, 70
  juvenile, 55
  see also custodial sentencing;
    incarceration
prison service, 65
  women in, 102
probation service, 59, 69
probation workers, 60, 73
  and inter-agency management, 66
problem youth, 19, 20, 22, 26
  age range of, 46, 49
  construction of, 35, 37
  representation of, 44–5
  see also youth, as problem
problems, definitions of, 28
prosecution, 66, 67, 74, 88
prostitution, 22, 103, 104, 106
  child, 10
psychiatry, 2, 85
psychology, 2, 15
public schools, 14
public spending, 64, 66
punishment, 48, 54, 59, 63, 88, 116, 118
  as basis of response to crime, 76
  in the community, 69, 70, 73
  and control, 21, 64
  culture of, 79, 82–3, 84, 93, 96, 114
  for hard core offenders, 67
  and sanctions, 81–2
  rather than treatment, 65
  and welfare, 60

punitiveness, 72, 80, 81, 97
  see also punishment, culture of

qualifications, in social work, 73
quality of life offences, 74, 94–5

race relations, 34, 43
racial minorities, 44, 45
rape, 95, 107
reality, and representation, 38–9, 41–3, 79
reciprocity, moral, 82
reconstruction
  postwar, 24–6, 28, 31, 34, 58, 115
  and social change, 33
Redwood, John, 80
reform, 14, 56–7, 69
Reform Schools, 55
reformers, middle class, 8–10
regulation, 51, 116
  of childhood, 10–11
  of the poor, 86, 87
  of working class, 13–14
  of youth, 14, 47, 67, 68
rehabilitation, 56–7, 63
reparation, 69, 75
  voluntary, 67
Reports
  Audit Commission (1996), 74, 75
  Curtis (1946), 57
  Ingleby (1960), 57
  Longford Study Group (1966), 58–9
  Molony (1933), 56
  pre-sentence, 70, 73
  social inquiry, 70
representation
  popular, and criminology, 115
  of problem youth, 44–5
  and reality, 38–9, 41–3, 79
research
  academic, and practical policies, 22, 76
  into causes of delinquency, 27–9
  lack of, 79
  and media representations, 40–1
  policy not based on, 66
residential care, 59, 63, 90

resistance, 34
responsibilities, of women, 102
responsibility, 65, 75
  age of criminal, 58, 59, 61, 83
  civic, 82
  social and individual, 64
revenge, and justice, 72, 73
rights
  of children in care, 90
  of citizens, 82–3
  human, 118
  of parents, 85, 86, 87
riots, 45, 47–8, 67, 71, 118
Rousseau, Jean-Jacques, 2

sanctions, and punishment, 81–2
scapegoating, 27, 41, 44, 93, 118
school, see education; public schools
Schools of criminology
  Birmingham, 31, 33
  Chicago, 21–3, 28
  Frankfurt, 39
science, 2, 20–1
secure training centres, 90
secure training orders, 71, 72, 81, 83
secure units, 92
sentencing
  and car crime, 71
  community based, 68–9
  custodial, 62, 66, 67
  and female offenders, 103
  non-custodial, 66, 67, 69
  related to offence, 69
sexuality
  and adolescence, 14–15
  of girls, 103, 106
  and innocence, 6–7
  of men, 108
shoplifting, 103, 104
short sharp shock, 57, 65, 66, 73
skinheads, 34
slum clearance, 31–2
social democracy, 23
social inquiry reports, 70
social order, 1, 9, 101, 118
  and regulation of childhood, 10–11
social progress, 28
social work, 21, 57, 58, 85

rejection of, 65
reorganization of, 62
women in, 102
social work intervention, 87
social work qualifications, 73
social workers, 58, 59, 60, 61, 63,
  83
  criticism of, 64, 85
  difficulties for, 62, 65
  and inter-agency management,
    66
  and paedophilia, 88
  and police work, 66–7
society, and media, 38–9
sociobiology, 27
spending, public, 64, 66
state
  authoritarian, 43
  and needs of citizens, 82–3
  see also welfare state
state control, 25
stereotypes, 16, 41, 103, 104
  of teenagers, 3
stop and search, 67
Straw, Jack, 75–6
street disorder, 13, 14
street robbery, 42–3
  see also mugging
subcultural theory, 23–4, 26, 28–9
subcultures, 32, 49
  delinquent, 23
  mods and rockers, 40–1
  oppositional, 35
  youth, 31, 33, 34
subjectivity, masculine, 109, 111
subversiveness, 26
supervision, 60, 63, 67
supervision orders, 62, 65, 66
surveillance, 67–8, 86
  by police, 40
surveys, victimization, 91–2

tabloids, 45, 64, 72, 76
teams, multi-agency, 75
teddy boys, 34, 44
teenagers
  poor male, 13
  stereotypes of, 3

theft, 3, 94
    from the person, 91
training, 56, 68, 74
    of criminal justice personnel, 70
treatment, 54, 57, 59, 65, 116
    disillusion with, 63–4
    flexible, 60
    intermediate, 63, 68
        intensive, 66
truancy, 56, 59, 68

unemployment, 3, 44, 45, 48, 115,
        117
United Nations Convention, Rights of
        the Child, 83
unrest, see disorder; industrial unrest

victim blaming, 27–8, 45, 92
victimization, 60
    perceptions of, 99
    of young people, 79, 82, 84, 91–2, 93,
        95, 117
        adults' indifference to, 96
        in care, 87–90
        in families, 84–7
victimization surveys, 91–2
victims, 74, 96
    adults as, 93–5
    males as, 111
    young people as, 56–7, 77, 90, 92,
        116
videos, violent, 2–3, 50–1, 115
violence, 3–4, 42, 67, 86, 90, 102
voices
    of criminal women, 105
    subordinated, 118
    of young people, 12, 28, 35, 119
        legitimized, 29
voluntary organizations, and inter-
        agency management, 66
vulnerability, 4, 92, 93, 94–5
    young people's, 95–6

Waddington, David, 70
warnings, and formal cautions, 75
welfare, 54, 63, 64, 70, 96, 106
    child, 84, 87
    disciplinary, 68

and individual needs, 69–70
    and punishment, 60
    social, 19, 76
    and social control, 61–2
    and youth justice, 54–61
welfare state, 26, 44, 115
Welsh Social Services Inspectorate,
        89–90
Willis, P., 35
womanhood, idealization of, 8, 9
women, 29, 94
    and control, 101–2
    and crime, 100, 102
    and criminology, 99–100, 103–6
    and male subordination, 108
    see also girls; offenders, female
working class community, 34
working class culture, 33
working class opinion, 61
working class, urban, regulation of,
        13–14
working class urban poor, surveillance
        of, 12
working class, white, 31, 110
    see also families, working class;
        youth, working class

Young, J., 41–2
Young Offender Courts, 59
young people
    attitudes to education, 92
    control of, 54, 56, 60, 77, 82
    harassment of, 91
    lower class, 23, 99
    and petty offending, 93, 94–5
    and petty/serious offending, 92
    supervision of, 60
    victimization of, 79
    as victims, 56–7, 77, 90, 95–6,
        116
    and vulnerability, 95–6
    see also childhood; children; girls;
        offenders; problem youth; youth
youth
    and affluence, 25–6
    as age of deviance, 3
    black, 44
    black male, 43

and citizenship, 68, 116, 118
and crime, 1, 11, 88, 107, 110–11,
      114, 117, 118, 119
   construction of, 54, 79, 95, 96,
      113, 115
and criminology, 18, 19–21, 23
and culture, 32
discourses of, 13, 16–17
as focus of anxiety, 43, 44, 46–7
male, 13, 43, 49, 98
and media, 40–1, 46–51
as 'other', 12, 20, 35, 96, 116
as outsiders, 74
as problem, 1, 14, 42, 77, 84, 96, 115,
      116
   public perception of, 38
seen as white male, 35

as social category, 24, 33, 37
working class, 14, 55
   see also childhood; children; girls;
      offenders; problem youth; young
      people
youth clubs, 48
Youth Courts, 70
youth culture, 33, 51
   and criminology, 18
youth justice
   and welfare, 53–61
   see also juvenile justice
youth service, 25
youth treatment centres, 63

Zero Tolerance (feminist), 74, 86
Zero Tolerance (policing), 74

UNDERSTANDING CRIME DATA
HAUNTED BY THE DARK FIGURE

Clive Coleman and Jenny Moynihan

- What are the main ways of acquiring numerical information about crime and offenders?
- How can we understand this information and avoid the various pitfalls of interpretation?
- What does the evidence tell us about the relationships between offending and age, sex, race, class, unemployment, and trends in crime over the years?

This clear and practical text breathes life into an essential subject that students have at times found uninspiring. It provides a guide to crime data for those with little background in the subject and at the same time, it will provide a source of reference for more experienced researchers. The authors have, for example, minimized as far as possible the presentation of detailed figures and complicated tables, but they have not avoided some of the more difficult issues that arise in interpreting and using such data.

Understanding crime data begins by locating the study and use of crime data within the theoretical and historical development of criminology, a subject that has long been haunted by the dark figure of hidden crime and offenders. Readers are guided through the development, limitations and uses of the three main sources of numerical crime data, and selected key issues in the interpretation of crime data are examined.

The characteristics of offenders are discussed with reference to the key variables of age, sex, race and class, and the difficulties involved in interpreting long- and short-term trends in the crime rate are highlighted. The authors assess what crime data can tell us about the relationships between crime and unemployment, and they conclude the book with their personal evaluation and prognosis of the field.

Understanding crime data is a well structured text for students of criminology, and it includes annotated further reading, lists of basic concepts, and a glossary for ease of reference. It will also have considerable appeal to professionals in criminal justice, probation and social work.

Contents
Haunted by the dark figure: criminologists as ghostbusters? – Official statistics: the authorized version? – Self-report studies: true confessions? – Victimization surveys: total recall? – Characteristics of offenders: the usual suspects? – Interpreting trends: quantum leaps? – Conclusion: carry on counting? – Glossary – References – Index

192pp   0 335 19518 0 (Paperback)   0 335 19519 9 (Hardback)

UNDERSTANDING JUSTICE
AN INTRODUCTION TO IDEAS, PERSPECTIVES AND CONTROVERSIES IN MODERN PENAL THEORY

Barbara Hudson

- Why should offenders be punished – what should punishments be designed to achieve?
- Why has imprisonment become the *normal* punishment for crime in modern industrial societies?
- What is the relationship between theories of punishment and the actual penalties inflicted on offenders?

Understanding justice is one of a series of student textbooks designed to cover the major areas of debate within the fields of criminology, criminal justice and penology. It provides a comprehensive account of the ideas and controversies that have arisen within law, philosophy, sociology and criminology about the punishment of criminals. Written in a clear, accessible style, it summarizes major philosophical ideas – retribution, rehabilitation, incapacitation – and discusses their strengths and weaknesses.

The sociological perspectives of Durkheim, the Marxists, Foucault and their contemporary followers are analysed and assessed. A section on the criminological perspective on punishment looks at the influence of theory on penal policy, and at the impact of penal ideologies on those on whom punishment is inflicted. The contributions of feminist theorists, and the challenges they pose to masculinist accounts of punishment, are included. The concluding chapter presents critiques of the very idea of punishment, and looks at contemporary proposals which could make society's response to crime less dependent on punishment than at present.

Understanding justice has been designed for students from a range of disciplines and is suitable for a variety of crime-related courses in sociology, social policy, law and social work. It will also be useful to professionals in criminal justice agencies and to all those interested in understanding the issues behind public and political debates on punishment.

Contents
Perspectives on punishment – Part 1: The goals of punishment: the judicial perspective – Utilitarian approaches – Retribution – Hybrids, compromises and syntheses – Part 2: Punishment and modernity: the sociological perspective – Punishment and progress: the Durkheimian tradition – The political economy of punishment: Marxist approaches – The disciplined society: Foucault and the analysis of penality – Part 3: Towards justice? – The struggle for justice: critical criminology and critical legal studies – Postscript: Beyond the modernity: the fate of justice – Glossary of key terms – Suggestions for further reading – References – Index.

192pp   0 335 19329 3 (Paperback)   0 335 19684 5 (Hardback)